CURACIES
TO SURVIVE THEM

Matthew Caminer
with
Martyn Percy and Beaumont Stevenson

Cartoons by Adrian Bradshaw-Jones

First published in Great Britain in 2015

Society for Promoting Christian Knowledge
36 Causton Street
London SW1P 4ST
www.spckpublishing.co.uk

British Library Cataloguing-in-Publication Data
A catalogue record for this book is available from the British Library

ISBN 978–0–281–07343–6
eBook ISBN 978–0–281–07344–3

Typeset by Graphicraft Limited, Hong Kong
First printed in Great Britain by Ashford Colour Press
Subsequently digitally printed in Great Britain

eBook by Graphicraft Limited, Hong Kong

Produced on paper from sustainable forests

Contents

*Dedicated to all those who have creatively
struggled both as curates and incumbents,
as did Jacob with his angel, to discover
a fuller identity*

Foreword

Eavesdropping on conversations is always tempting. This time you should give in to the temptation. Matthew Caminer, clergy spouse and management consultant, Beau Stevenson, priest and psychotherapist, and Martyn Percy, for ten years principal of a theological college, bring a wealth of experience to the complex question of training curacies. The result is an authentic, instructive and entertaining conversation about the path from ordination as a deacon to becoming a priest and a vicar.

It is easy to be anecdotal about 'how it was in my day' and critical of education and development in today's world. The profile of candidates and incumbents has radically changed in the last 25 years. Former stereotypes of the curate as young, male and white no longer apply. Modern-day working agreements, policy documents and modern management are simple targets, when things go wrong. The authors do focus on where things go wrong, while acknowledging that many curacies go well and that tight corners can be the making of us. The book's strength is that in so doing it highlights points of learning. The case studies take us below the surface to examine the complex and paradoxical dynamics in relationship, vocation and authority structures.

I was not surprised to read that most of the respondents in the underlying survey asked to remain anonymous. One of the most difficult issues in a training curacy is often the conspiracy of silence. There is a reluctance to name problems as they arise, whether it be curate talking to incumbent, incumbent to curate, or either one to the diocesan officer, archdeacon or bishop. The reluctance is understandable and often stems from the best of motives. Some are blind to the early problems. Others hope that it is a temporary blip and that things will improve. Many are wary of being misunderstood or seen as 'trouble' by bishop or archdeacon.

The book tellingly breaks the silence. The vignettes are perceptive – sometimes amusing, sometimes heartbreaking – sketches which, taken seriously, throw into relief what is happening underneath the surface. They challenge, for example, diocese, parish, incumbent and curate to check whether a policy of 'wait and see' is godly wisdom or an approach that runs the risk that the situation will escalate to a point of pastoral breakdown. Where curacies do run into difficulties the authors encourage us to serious reflection and mature action rather than 'letting off steam' to friends or colleagues or keeping a private record in case there is trouble.

In holding up such a mirror to us, there may, of course, be some discomfort. As they peel the layers from the onion, the authors do not claim infallible judgements but offer thought-provoking insights to make us have a closer look at how we relate as individual clergy and within the corporate body of the Church. Like all overheard conversations, you are likely to find yourself wanting to join in, sometimes strongly agreeing, sometimes disagreeing. The questions at the end of each chapter positively invite us to do just that. Treated superficially, these mini-questionnaires may seem as mechanistic as some of the policy documents for curacies. If we stop there, we do less than justice to the authors' desire to ensure that all such tools are used as living documents by diocese and local church. I hope that many will take the trouble to follow them up.

At the heart of every curacy for curate and incumbent is that sense of God's call – and at its heart is the deceptively simple call to live out our faith following the footsteps of Jesus. It is usually harder than we expect but more rewarding than our wildest dreams. It is always worth deeper reflection and prayer. You will find food for this journey here.

Sheila Watson
Archdeacon of Canterbury

Acknowledgements

This book couldn't have come about without the contributions of many training incumbents and curates, past and present. The fact that they are not named does not diminish our gratitude to them for their being prepared to be vulnerable, frank and open. Thanks also to Archdeacon Sheila for her Foreword, and to Alison and everyone at SPCK for their wisdom and guidance; to all our friends at Ripon College Cuddesdon for hosting our meetings, and to everyone who has helped by reviewing the text, making suggestions and above all encouraging us in this project. Finally, a special thank you to Adrian Bradshaw-Jones for the cartoons which appear from time to time to exercise the other side of our brains, thereby helping us to work our way through some fairly meaty topics.

About the authors

Matthew Caminer is an independent management consultant specializing in process improvement. In addition to his professional work, he is a writer and speaker, regularly leading workshops for vocation seekers and ordinands, with their spouses, for theological colleges and dioceses. Matthew has been a diocesan work consultant, a consultant to parish teams, and a coach and mentor in the workplace. His first book was *A Clergy Husband's Survival Guide* (SPCK, 2012).

The Very Revd Professor Martyn William Percy is Dean of Christ Church, Oxford. He was from 2004 to 2014 Principal of Ripon College Cuddesdon, one of the world's leading Anglican theological colleges. A member of the Faculty of Theology at the University of Oxford, Martyn writes and teaches on modern ecclesiology. His recent books include *Anglicanism: Confidence, Commitment and Communion* (Ashgate, 2013) and *Thirty-Nine New Articles: An Anglican Landscape of Faith* (Canterbury Press, 2013).

The Revd Canon Beaumont Stevenson is Pastoral Care Advisor to the Diocese of Oxford, a member of the Institute of Group Analysis and a practising psychotherapist. He helped co-found the Introductory Course in Group Analysis, and taught Pastoral Psychology at St Stephen House, Oxford. For many years he was Senior Chaplain of the psychiatric hospitals of Oxford and a member of the staff support team. As former diocesan training officer, he has a particular interest in helping clergy teams identify their common sense of vocation.

Introduction

Curacies and How to Survive Them may sound like an invitation to watch and listen while we explore strategies for escaping the gloom, failure and despondency that are presumably endemic in curacies. The real state of curacies is a little different. You only need to talk to people who have completed them to see that for many it is plain sailing and more, something to celebrate. Here's a flavour:[1]

'I had a great curacy. My training incumbent was supportive and encouraging and did a great job.'

'The freedom to discover my own way to be! Curacy has been less prescriptive than I anticipated and this has been a joy!'

'My curacy was the making of me.'

'Confirmation that I am in the right place, that so many people say to me "to the manor born", I was called to be a priest. It's just awesome.'

'Taking Holy Communion, taking funerals, being a part of a church family who love me and I them.'

The list could continue, but even these few insights make the point: for the three years that most curacies last, the partnership between the curate and the training incumbent is often a very positive experience and a blessing to all involved.

Even the curacies described above will have had their ups and downs: that is normal in any training relationship. Sadly, however, some take a different course:

'Denied opportunities to gain experience, not given adequate pastoral oversight or support by the training incumbent and told that, as a curate is only around for three or four years, I wasn't a real member of the team.'

'Lack of support from incumbent. Lack of any support from the diocese even though they knew things were difficult.'

'Abused, threatened and bullied!'

We will look at examples of the problems experienced during curacies as we go through the book, but there is little doubt that they exist, and of their consequences. It was a frequently recurring theme when I was researching my book for clergy husbands,[2] and a recent book that tracks the experiences of curacies[3] supports this: 'Unfortunately, some curacies encounter difficulties, despite the best of intentions . . . you do not have to travel far in the Church of England to find a story about a difficult curacy.'

Many of the problems encountered during curacies are temporary and surmountable learning experiences from which everyone benefits. Occasionally, though, the situations are disturbing for everyone involved and require intervention, separation of the people concerned, or even serious decisions about future ministry. Even when it is only a transient phase, the experience can feel extremely uncomfortable at the time. If the curacy then takes a wrong turn, a lot of effort may be required to turn the situation round, and then not before there has been emotional fall-out. Tim Ling grounds curacies in this reality, describing a complex transition from the life before to the life after ordination:[4]

> Anglican priesthood is at the same time deeply personal and irreducibly corporate; it is shaped by context but subject ultimately only to God. Little wonder that new entrants to the 'clerical profession' find themselves challenged by questions of authority, identity, ambiguity and practice.

Although difficulties in curacies are by no means a new phenomenon, the context for today's Church and the way it operates is in a period of very rapid evolution. The demographic mix of those offering themselves for ordination has undergone a major shift, and new models of parish ministry are emerging to reflect changing attitudes to organized religion, falling numbers, depleted funding and a renewed emphasis on mission.

In the meantime, the combined influence of the Hind Report and Common Tenure, along with the relaunch of Post-Ordination Training as IME4-7,[5] has resulted in new processes and new ways of thinking that colour all aspects of curacies. Like any changes, these take time to get used to, but some people have described the new approaches as prescriptive, over-engineered and mechanistic, with a strong touch of one-size-fits-all, overlaid with a skewed academic emphasis. The approaches are sometimes seen as bureaucratic, requiring extra work by training incumbents, while placing an increased burden on already stretched diocesan staff. For some newly ordained curates and their training incumbents, they induced a sense of 'panic and disbelief', as one curate put it, so soon after the euphoria of the service of ordination.

The Church is not indifferent to this, as demonstrated by ongoing work under the banner Resourcing Ministerial Education; and, in 2014, Ministry Division issued a report[6] on the selection and training of training incumbents in recognition that things were not as they should be, that urgent action was required, and certainly rejecting a default assumption that if a curacy goes wrong it must be the curate's fault. Simultaneously, individual dioceses were taking their own steps to realign the training of curates to what would work and what is needed, learning from the first few years' experience of implementing IME4–7. The Bishop of Dorchester observed:

> There is a desire to help those moving into incumbencies in particular (which is, of course, only some priests) to be as well prepared as possible for doing so. One who did that recently, coming from a teaching background, described that experience was the equivalent of an NQT (newly qualified teacher) moving into a headship in a single leap. I think that that is rather an exaggeration but it has been very sad to see many good priests out of their depth when they become incumbents.

Certainly it has been part of my hope in overseeing the IME 4–7 work to support both those who are making that transition (and the lack of second curacy posts is a definite problem here) and those who are not (and there remains a fundamental confusion because of the tendency to equate being priests with being vicars).

Whether we are actually succeeding in this aim is something I don't think that we will be able to assess for a good few years to come – but I still think that the effort is well worth making given all the known difficulties that there have been in the past.

Despite best endeavours such as these, the design of the process and the way it is implemented at national, diocesan and parish levels, continues to have mixed success. For some, whether curates or training incumbents, or both, it can be a negative experience, sometimes with repercussions that outlast the term of the curacy.

The shifting environment does not by itself explain the phenomenon of troubled curacies. This raises questions that lie at the heart of this book. Taking as a given that curacies do sometimes get into difficulties, is this the result of normal growing pains or are there more fundamental issues? What are the underlying causes, and what could be done to mitigate them to help future curates and training incumbents?

'My curate doesn't understand me'

To answer these questions I needed some help. I turned to two people. The Revd Canon Beaumont Stevenson is Pastoral Care Advisor for the Diocese of Oxford. His work as a psychotherapist also includes counselling clergy and their spouses. The Very Revd Professor Martyn Percy, Dean of Christ Church, Oxford, was for ten years (from 2004 to 2014) Principal of Ripon College Cuddesdon – one of the largest training colleges for clergy in the Church of England. I asked them both for their perspectives:

Beau If you needed proof that curacies get into difficulty, you only need to look at my appointments book. Curates and training incumbents regularly come to people like me for help, either self-referred or sent by the diocese.

The Church is in a constant tension, a mix of excitement and frustration that church communities grow into over time. I'll talk more about that later, but when a curate comes along, new to the environment, going through multiple upheavals, and still enjoying the post-ordination glow, those same tensions can be challenging and at times feel insurmountable. That's why so many of them end up in the consulting room or seeking help elsewhere.

Matthew If the dynamics are so challenging and the tensions so clear, then surely the groundwork for this could be laid much earlier in the process, as part of the training and, especially, formation prior to ordination.

'My incumbent doesn't understand me'

Martyn The Kiliva people of Papua New Guinea have a word, *mokita*, that expresses what everyone knows but nobody says.[7] As far as curacies go, the *mokita* is the frequency with which problems, many of them avoidable, arise in curacies; and the tendency almost to collude in a determination *not* to talk about them. I have heard many stories, some of them quite harrowing, from former students demonstrating that there really is a problem. A lot of the problems start at the beginning of curacies, especially the choice of title post,[8] or even earlier. We try to give our students and their families – very important! – as realistic an idea as we can of the life they should expect. The emerging challenge is that more and more of the training and formation for ordination is on a part-time basis or by distance learning, so this task will become even harder in the future.

Matthew One thing that the three of us share, therefore, is the experience of coming face to face with people who have troubled stories to tell. It is not usually appropriate for either the hierarchy of the Church or the congregations to know the details: they are often left in ignorance while the protagonists maintain a professional silence and an outwardly serene demeanour. But that serves only to intensify the impact of what is going on beneath the surface.

So what are we trying to do in this book and how have we gone about exploring problem curacies?

In short, we want to help. We do this in two ways. First, we explore the dynamics and psychology of the critically important relationship between the curate and the training incumbent. This is intended to help the people involved to recognize signs of impending difficulty and take appropriate action, including seeking the right kind of help in good time. Second, because many of the issues that arise are rather more prosaic, for instance areas like work organization, time management and administration, we offer practical solutions that can deliver immediate benefits.

At the heart of *Curacies and How to Survive Them* are eight conversations between the three authors: Martyn, an educator, Beau, a therapist, and Matthew, a management consultant joining in and prodding the conversation along. These explore a selection of situations that are often found in curacies, presented in the form of case studies.

The content of these case studies is derived from research carried out in 2013–14 via an online survey to which there were contributions from over 50 self-selected curates and training incumbents from 17 dioceses.

If you seek answers that are unequivocal, you may be disappointed. Paradox is present to a greater or lesser extent in all the case studies, so things that look as if they should converge or coincide seem to have features that are mutually exclusive or counter-intuitive. Thus the apparently perfect and uneventful curacy may by its very serenity be missing something. Similarly, an apparently career-threatening bust-up between the curate and the training incumbent in the middle of the curacy may be the very making of them.

Throughout the data-gathering a common feature was the extreme reluctance of the respondents to be identified. In some cases this was even expressed in terms suggesting that their identification might be career-threatening. This has been respected by describing the stories, the situations and the people involved in fictionalized form, an approach that also made it possible to amalgamate converging but nuanced themes into composite case studies. No individual person's story has been told, so if you believe you can identify your particular experience, it serves only to confirm that many of these situations are encountered relatively frequently.

There are several ways that the reader may consider using the case studies, the conversations and the questions that follow. As well as working through the book individually, readers may wish to use the case studies as the basis for group discussion before going back to the text and seeing where our conversation led us.

Whichever approach you take, you may reach conclusions and ask questions that differ from ours, developing your own list of key issues and questions. You may have gone on to start the process of devising answers to those questions – and then the case studies will certainly have served their purpose, and so will the book.

THE CONVERSATIONS

1

The nightmare curate

It is tempting to make three assumptions about problem curacies: first, that it is always the curate who is the victim; second, that many of the problems are transient in nature and can be resolved; and third, that the curate is the right person in the right place. But what if none of those assumptions is true, even to the extent that the curate should not have been ordained in the first place?

In any selection process there is bound to be a certain incidence of false positives (those who receive a positive outcome but should not have been approved) and false negatives (those who receive a negative outcome but should have been approved). But should we accept the inevitability of these poor decisions? Let's pause and have a look at this.

We can never know how many people consider a vocation, whether as a fleeting thought that is as quickly dismissed, or as a prompting that won't go away. What we can say, though, is that each year between 700 and 800[1] people go to a Bishops' Advisory Panel (BAP), the pivotal stage in the Church of England's process of discernment of new vocations. Of these about 80 per cent are thought to be recommended for training, though we do not know how many of them end up being ordained, let alone complete a first curacy. The process contains many opportunities for reflection and assessment, by the Church and by the individual, and there is a certain amount of attrition. What we might reasonably expect, therefore, is that this notoriously drawn-out discernment process would filter out any false positives, reducing the risk of someone inappropriate reaching a live parish context.

Some may feel that this risk could be reduced by addressing the 80 per cent approval rate, which sounds very high indeed, but this figure needs to be seen in context.

The sequence of activities from an initial sense of a possible vocation through to a diocesan decision whether to send the candidate on a BAP is deliberately drawn out. The candidate will no doubt have done a lot of thinking, probably in discussion with their parish priest. It is to be hoped that they will have discussed it with their family too, given the repercussions for all involved. There follows a succession of meetings over an extended period with vocations advisors and directors of ordinands, usually culminating in meeting the bishop. This process gives the opportunity to assess the gifts offered to the Church by the candidate against the realities of ordained life and the actual needs of the Church; and all this is done in the context of the nine criteria[2] that all candidates must satisfy in order to get a green light at the BAP. There are no quotas: at a BAP they are looking to see whether the person does or does not satisfy the criteria – most profoundly, perhaps, in the form of a clear vocation to the priesthood, but also in more practical areas.

One might assume that by the time the bishop makes the yes/no decision about whether to send the candidate to a BAP the likely outcome is clear. On that basis, 80 per cent actually seems a surprisingly low figure. It is not the prime purpose of this book to explore this in greater depth, though the whole area of false positives, and indeed of false negatives, might be something that Ministry Division could fruitfully research, given its huge investment both in the selection process and in the training that follows.

Let's stop thinking in statistics and abstract terms, and look at the potential impact when a curate who appears totally in-appropriate, for whatever reasons, takes up a title post. Margaret, a highly experienced training incumbent in a busy urban parish, tells her story.

I have always enjoyed being a training incumbent. It feels a privilege to accompany someone on perhaps the most difficult part of their journey, from newly ordained to wherever their ministry is going to take them next. As you might expect, I have seen all sorts and for the most part these have been times of joy, excitement and blessing. The congregation has always viewed the arrival of a new curate with eager anticipation, and contributed to making them feel welcome and part of the family. Nobody expects it all to be plain sailing, of course: that wouldn't be reasonable. For myself I have found that the on-going training that I also need to undertake to do my job properly can be a bit onerous on top of all my other work in the parish, but that hasn't stopped me doing what was asked of me; and some of the box-ticking that seems to be all the rage nowadays seems to take a lot of time without adding a whole lot. When it comes to the curates themselves, yes, naturally there are ups and downs. They are, after all, going through a major transition, and sometimes they have family things to sort out too. By the end of it all, though, we can usually take a look back with amusement at things that seemed so serious at the time, reminisce with a laugh about the mistakes and gaffes, and about the verbal fisticuffs which invariably happen some-where along the line.

But Brian . . . Oh dear!

I had already wondered why he had looked for a title post outside his own sponsoring diocese. I suppose I should have seen the signs at the initial interview. I thought we had done it right, and I went through my mental checklist and gave him the opportunity to ask questions, look around, meet people and everything else that would have shown him whether or not he could be comfortable and fulfilled among us. For our part, we listened, asked our own questions and came to a balanced conclusion. Yes, he seemed to interrupt a bit and he seemed a bit blustery, but I put that down to nerves and exploring the unknown. In a funny sort of way, though, he seemed almost a bit too well prepared, arriving with a long list of questions which at times seemed more to resemble the demands of a union shop steward than the basis for a frank and open exploration of whether this was the right thing for both of us.

Yes: that's it!

It was as if it was all about him, rather than something that would affect us all. It was not so much the questions, perhaps, but the tone in which they were asked, or his gestures, or the look on his face, so that while his words might have been agreeing with something I'd said, his inscrutable expression suggested that he might be thinking something quite different.

Anyway, the first big shock came only three days after he arrived. He wasn't due to be licensed for another ten days, but we'd arranged things so he could settle in without any commitments for a few days. That day, one of the churchwardens popped round with a homemade loaf, just one of many friendly gestures from the congregation, only to find the house empty and the key in the lock. All there was to show that he had ever been there was a note on the kitchen table: 'I can't possibly live in a house like this. It's far too near the main road for me to go to sleep at night, and the whole place is absolutely filthy. I hope you manage to find someone else.'

Extraordinary!

I was so glad that it was the churchwarden and not one of the other parishioners who made this discovery, after all the hard work to make the house ready for him. To cut a long story short, the bishop contacted him and read the riot act. I had real misgivings about letting him return, but the details hadn't leaked and the bishop persuaded me that my extensive experience might be just what was needed to turn things round. Brian returned, albeit reluctantly and without remorse, and the licensing went ahead as planned.

The truth is, though, that even with my very best efforts, I couldn't get round a basic thing about Brian. Everything was all about him. His vision. His view of how things should be run. What sort of churchmanship we should be moving towards. Believe it or not, he even started criticizing my sermons, and making 'helpful' comments about how I ran PCC meetings. And as for the training that he was meant to be doing, he wouldn't be taught. I know it was a huge transition from his previous career as an HR director, but it was almost as if I was the trainee and he thought he was the boss. Although he went through the motions of getting alongside people, he had no empathy at all, and people would come to me, sometimes in tears, because they had been made to feel as if the problems for which they were seeking counsel were of their own making and that they should 'just pull themselves together' – words that were reported back to me more than once.

Then, during my regular meeting at the Church of England primary school, the head teacher expressed strong misgivings about Brian's ability to interact with children. She said that her fellow staff also found him a very difficult person to work with, and there was always an atmosphere of discouragement in the staffroom when Brian had been visiting. I asked if he might improve with time and greater experience, but she thought this very unlikely.

Any of these things taken individually might have been manageable, but when I looked at them all together I realized that my greater responsibility was to the congregation and the parish, and now was the time for action. I telephoned the bishop and Brian left not long afterwards. I don't know what happened to him, but I hope he found happiness wherever he ended up. In the meantime, I was left to pick up the pieces.

Matthew Well, all I can say is, poor Margaret! Was Brian ill or simply a pain in the neck?

Beau It's sometimes hard to tell the difference, especially as these things are often a matter of degree. But when someone has such a distorted sense of reality and of their position in that reality, you do begin to wonder. On the basis of Margaret's story, Brian would certainly seem to be someone on the spectrum of narcissistic personality disorder. The trouble with this condition, like many others, is that it can be hard to spot in a short meeting like an interview; and, as Margaret observed, it could simply have been that Brian was overcompensating for nerves on the day. With conditions like these, life can progress without problems for years at a time, perhaps because everyone is to an extent on a spectrum of something: there's no such thing as 'normal'. Symptoms of this syndrome or that condition can simply come across as being a bit odd or socially difficult. Seen positively, they may appear like Tigger-like enthusiasm and energy. For most of us, taking account of the differences between individuals and their personalities is just part of the rough and tumble of interacting with people at work, in their families, among their friends.

'I've come to preach the gospel of ME'

Matthew But this is an extreme case. How on earth did Brian get anywhere near a parish?

Martyn I wish it were not so, but I have come across cases like Brian's, though fortunately not very often. I think Beau hit upon the problem when he said that these things are hard to spot in a short meeting. The journey to ordination involves a lot of different people taking part in short conversations. Although there is a paper trail, the conversations don't always join up. Familiarity can also lull people into ignoring factors that should be clamouring for attention. Even at a BAP, where the selectors are working with more or less a clean sheet of paper, there can be the tendency to assume the positive, precisely because they know the candidate has already been through so many hoops to get there.

Looking back, and with the benefit of hindsight, there are several things that could have happened. Listening to the way Brian went about negotiating and relating to people, I suppose, it is possible that his bishop knew all along that he wouldn't be a good fit but in the face of his strong personality found it difficult to say 'no'. Some bishops are not good at straight talking, and tend to rely, perhaps a little too heavily, on the BAP process to decide against a candidate. But if the bishop is of the conflict-aversive type (and there are some like this), problems can arise during the training process and beyond should the BAP recommend for training a candidate about whom the bishop had some unsurfaced, unprocessed and unarticulated reservations.

Matthew Does that really happen?

Martyn Oh yes. But even when it does happen, a successful outcome at a BAP does not automatically mean that the person will eventually be ordained, so there was already at least one further safety net already in place, though I suppose you could ask how they had got as far as a BAP in the first place. We'll never know. At the end of the training, the bishop is sent a report by the theological institution, usually a recommendation to ordain.

As principal of a theological college, I occasionally came to the conclusion that I could not recommend the ordination of a candidate, but it was the bishop's final decision whether or not to ordain the person. To be honest, though, it is usually the candidates who discover that this is not the right direction for them and they tend to make their own decision to withdraw from the training, so I didn't often find myself in that difficult position.

Matthew So there is indeed natural attrition at every stage of the process, including between a BAP and ordination.

Martyn Yes, indeed, although a decision to withdraw is more often taken because of illness, family circumstances or difficulty with the academic requirements, not because of a fundamental mismatch on this scale. But even in a case like Brian's, I have known instances where I have recommended that a candidate should not go forward to ordination, but the bishop has overridden that recommendation, just as it is within a bishop's prerogative to override a negative decision at a BAP.

Where the ordinand is a residential student at theological college, it is relatively easy to observe them, of course, not just in the formal setting of classes and seminars but also in how they fit in within the community. It is something of a 24/7 existence, and the word formation refers to something a great deal broader than their understanding of the Bible or their knowledge of Church history and canon law. It is about the whole person. Thus, for someone like Brian to reach the end of his studies and get a positive final report from the principal is certainly not just a pat on the head simply for sticking it out for three years.

On the other hand, more and more ordination training is by distance learning, or is done on a part-time basis. We tried to offer a formational dimension to this, but with such limited exposure to the ordinands that is a much greater challenge. So, with reluctance, I have to agree that whichever route ordinands like Brian take through training it is still possible for them to get all the way through, from vocation-seeking to ordination, without anyone deeply questioning the suitability of their personality or character. They may have ticked lots of other boxes, but more latent reservations about an individual may not have had time to gestate and mature.

Matthew Do you think that is what happened in Brian's case?

Martyn Well, of course, this is a fictionalized story, but it resonates with shades of truth from many different situations that have come across my desk.

Matthew So maybe he shouldn't have got this far, but he did. So what happened on the interview day, Beau?

Beau It sounds to me as if Margaret, the training incumbent, and those around her had covered all the bases. Isn't it interesting, though, to observe the danger signals?

- Brian's choice of a title post outside his own diocese. Doesn't this suggest that they knew him all too well, and had released him, to use the jargon?
- His long and over-elaborate list of questions.
- His lack of recognition, let alone acknowledgement, of what the host parish had done to make the meeting easy.
- The apparent spirit of judgement in the way he assessed what he saw and heard.
- Above all, the sense that it was all about him, and him alone.

If I have any criticism of Margaret it is that she didn't give these warning signs more attention. But that is easy to say, I know. The dynamics were clearly at odds from the beginning: Margaret seeking to pave the way for frank, open and objective discussions, Brian doing everything possible to control the high ground and set the agenda.

Matthew Yes, I can think of people for whom I have had to adapt my behaviour and expectations to make things work between us, and I am quite certain that people have frequently had to do the same with me! But although you mentioned a specific condition, Beau, isn't it more often just a question of jarring personality types and therefore a shared responsibility to understand one other and adapt accordingly, perhaps along the lines of Myers-Briggs, Enneagram, Belbin or any of the other personality profile tools?

Beau Yes, I suppose the word 'disorder' may sound a bit alarming, and saying that we are all 'on the spectrum of something or other' may seem a little unhelpful. But I think it was Ursula Le Guin who said, 'What sane person could live in this world and not be crazy?'

It's really just using different words for the same observation. After all, somebody with particular Myers-Briggs characteristics may well be 'on the spectrum of something', but at such a low level that most of us accommodate it without ever thinking about it.

Matthew I sometimes think that in the church we may bend over a little further than in some other environments to accommodate these differences and the people at the extremes. Perhaps we respond to the gospel imperative to love one another in a way that may blind us to what is there in front of us, regardless of the inevitable pitfalls. For example, I was once the director of a church music group. An adult member of the congregation wanted to play the cello in the group even though her playing was simply awful! The vicar urged me to accept the 'precious gift' that she was offering, a gift that was far more important than the technicality of whether or not she could actually play in tune and in time. The result was that everyone had to compensate, but even then the overall sound deteriorated to the extent that instead of facilitating worship it impeded it by pulling the attention of the congregation. In case you think I am being a musical snob, I also remember acting as a steward at a great festival for the deaf in Coventry Cathedral. In purely musical terms, the sound of 2,000 deaf people singing was a cacophony, but in all other senses, and of course the sense that mattered, it was the music of angels. The first decision could be seen as colluding to deny the truth that this was plain wrong; the second was us colluding to celebrate what needed to be celebrated. Where does Brian's case lie between these extremes?

Martyn Every candidate for ordination is different. Not only that, but as they travel along the journey from, say, first being aware of the need to explore the vocation to arriving in a parish as a curate, each individual candidate changes almost beyond recognition. After all, some people describe a journey that has taken 20 years or more, during which time they may have gone through many major life events – the joy of marriage, the grief of bereavement, parenthood, redundancy, among others. All these have an impact on the individual. Even without them, as we travel our day-to-day journey we evolve. Spiritually it is the same. People's spiritual lives have a rich, dense, organic texture, and that changes over times and seasons. We are shaped in our spiritual journeys by a lengthy and broad range of encounters and events. And by God, who changes us both within and without these encounters and events.

We tend to get a little wiser as we get older, and this can then help to put the extremes of highs and lows into better perspective. We have mountain-top experiences and we have times in the desert. At times we can barely glimpse any vestige of the truth, let alone seeing through a glass darkly, while at other times we can be almost exultant with certainty.

In other words, the person the vocation advisor meets for the first time is a completely different person from the curate who arrives in a parish a number of years later. I'm not talking here about the different views of what it is to be a priest, whether ontological or qualified, Mary or Martha, High Church or Evangelical, liturgical or mission-focused, or whatever. Even where those positions remain fixed for the individual, the way people understand them and express them can evolve. And, of course, they may also alter radically. Is it any wonder that Margaret wondered which version of Brian was going to come into the room each morning?

Matthew So are you saying that these extremes are natural and that we should always find a way of working around the eccentricities, foibles and dysfunctionalities of each new curate, because by definition they are all different and all have their plus and minus points?

Martyn No. I think Beau would agree that there comes a point when those eccentricities, foibles and dysfunctionalities are so extreme that they take on greater significance and militate against the greater good, the need for a priest to be able to serve, interact, lead from behind and live and preach the gospel. If they cannot do that without wrecking the peace, and are not able to respond to attempts to help them, then there may indeed be no place for them in public ministry.

Matthew That's all very well. But not everyone shows visible signs of this or that condition. Some people are just plain bolshie; they won't be told, and they can't take criticism. Shouldn't we find a way of accommodating them?

Beau You're not painting a different picture here, Matthew, just underlining the fact that it's all a matter of degree and it depends on how you look on it. Even granting that we cannot ignore the training incumbent's contribution to the dynamic between the two, there does come the point when it is unreasonable to expect the training incumbent to take all the responsibility for making the curacy work. If the curate cannot or will not recognize his or her role in doing so, but instead continues to behave as the 'nightmare curate', then it has to stop.

Matthew So, we're not to walk the extra mile?

Martyn Oh yes, we are, but by helping the curate to find the best context for his or her ministry, which may after all not be in the Church at all; it may still be as valid a vocation, just a calling to do something different. That is why the Church promotes spiritual direction for all clergy, as well as mediation, work consultants, pastoral advisors, peer groups and retreats. The curate should not be alone while discerning anew a way forward; neither, if it gets as bad as this, should the curate be allowed to jeopardize the mission of the Church, which must always be the greater responsibility.

And there's another aspect of this. When we think about bully-ing, it might be natural to assume that it is usually the training incumbent who is the bully and the curate the victim. The relationship between Margaret and Brian amply demonstrates the potential for the curate to be a bully.

Matthew It sounds as if you are getting ready to tie a millstone round Brian's neck!

Martyn I am quite sure that's how Margaret felt at times. Seriously, though, the tragedy is that in these cases it is actually more common for it to go untreated, in the same way that everyone may know that a person has a drinking problem but be reluctant to intervene. Thus a nightmare curate may complete their three-year term and be let loose as a vicar with their own parish; and, heaven forbid, they may even become a training incumbent. The risks are too great for this to be allowed to happen.

Matthew I think I am a little confused. Are we saying that the Brians of this world have no place in the Church and shouldn't have got this far in the first place, or that we have to find a way of working that uses their skills and limits the damage they do?

Beau You're not going to like this, Matthew, but the answer is both. As you will see as we go through these conversations, just about every situation represents a dichotomy. Yes, we must seek to protect the greater good, and I agree that we should be better at reducing the number of false negatives and false positives. But when St Paul writes of the different parts of the body each having a role to play, that confronts us with the need to accommodate priests who are not clones, but reflect the whole array of genders, sexualities and personality types, just as we celebrate different theologies, and find roles for the ministry of people with debilitating medical conditions.

Matthew So, even if curates like Brian are the stuff of nightmares, are we saying that we always have a shared responsibility to find a way through? Certainly the questions at the end of the chapter and the tips at the end of the book may help us to do so, but I think we need some clarification about where to draw the line between acceptance of the so-called 'nightmare curate', and the need to take direct action.

'... my cup runneth over'

Martyn I think nightmares come in many shapes and sizes. A nightmare is essentially an unpleasant dream that often causes strong emotional responses in the mind. Typically these may consist of horror, fear, stress, despair, anxiety – or a deep sadness. A person who has had a nightmare will often awake in a state of distress. No person is 'a nightmare', clearly. And a curate cannot be one either. What matters, therefore, is changing the person's behaviour pattern. If this can't be altered, then more radical adjustments may be needed – a change to the curate's ministry, for example.

Matthew So Margaret did the right thing, persevering to give Brian the best opportunity to shine, gathering her facts, taking soundings and eventually contacting the bishop?

Beau Yup!

Points for reflection

Curates

- What expectations and assumptions do you have about your curacy and the life of ministry?
- If you have a family, how much have you discussed the impact on them of the life of ministry?
- What is your understanding of your ordination vows?

Training incumbents

- How well prepared are you in interviews with prospective curates to understand the underlying personality issues that may colour the curacy relationship?
- What expectations and assumptions colour your working relationship with your new curate?
- How robust is your own support mechanism so that when – not if – frustrations arise you can share them in an appropriate and helpful environment?

Dioceses

- Going right back to the beginning of the journey to a curacy, how certain are you that the right people are being sent to BAPs, and why do you think that only 80 per cent are recommended for training in spite of the extended process of screening and discernment?
- How proactive are you in ensuring that the right curates end up in the right title posts?
- What training do you give to prospective training incumbents and parishes in the skills need for successful interviewing and selection?
- How do you deploy work consultants at the beginning of a curacy, assuming you have such a scheme?
- When things go pear-shaped, what procedures do you have in place, and what is the balance between policy and pastoral responses?

2

Yes, because it's policy

Whether curates are the stuff of nightmares or paragons, they still need to be trained. Let's look at the impact of a one-size-fits-all approach to training and formation in the context of a curacy.

This takes two forms. The first is the enduring assumption that the default outcome of curacy training will be a position of responsibility in full-time stipendiary ministry. The reality is that this is less and less the case; indeed, the emergence of new 'minster models' with large numbers of parishes linked in ever-growing benefices demonstrates quite the opposite trend. A future reality is likely to comprise a decreasing number of full-time stipendiary priests, mostly male,[1] supported by teams of mostly self-supporting and/or locally ordained ministers and licensed lay ministers, many of them women. Although this diversity is, to an extent, reflected in the availability of different learning path options and additional modules, expectations and assumptions have not yet caught up.

The second symptom of a one-size-fits-all approach is the perception of a narrow, formulaic and rigid training regime that is sometimes perceived by curates as disempowering, or even infantilizing. One example of this is an inflexible requirement in some dioceses to work towards a degree or a doctorate. Curates are, after all, often people who are entering the Church with excellent academic qualifications, or after a distinguished first career, offering the Church an incredibly rich mixture of academic, professional and spiritual experience, intellect and vocations.

Rick's story shows how the combination of the default assumption about ministry and rigid approaches to learning paths can result in a toxic curacy.

It was time for the annual review. Rick listened in stunned silence.

'You know, I just can't train you. You seem to be obsessed with chaplaincy work and won't do what you are meant to be doing at St Anselm's. And even worse, you have no sense of obedience when it comes to the academic work you are meant to be doing. I simply can't understand how anyone could not have a passion for parish ministry. Come to that, it may be painful to hear this, but I sometimes wonder why they ordained you.'

Rick's equilibrium was badly shaken as he considered his training incumbent's assertions, especially given that they had not been discussed in earlier supervision sessions. Eventually he replied.

'Can we take the two things separately? I have been a lay chaplain for 15 years. It was the head chaplain at the Royal County Hospital Group who encouraged me to explore ordination, and I discussed it at length, prayed about it and did everything I could to make sure it was the right thing to do. There was complete transparency about my vocation. You and I discussed it at length before St Anselm's was chosen as my title post. Yes, I've heard people snigger that I have chosen to go for second-class ministry, whatever they mean by that, but it never occurred to me that you would be one of them, and I find it highly demotivating and discouraging that you should speak in those terms.'

He waited for a response, but instead there was silence. Rick continued.

'All the time I was doing my work as a hospital chaplain, I was fully involved in the church and with the vicar's encouragement I did some formal study, and if you have another look at my CV you'll remember that I have a PhD in theology, as well as having done a number of specific study modules that are accredited by the diocese under the portfolio scheme. So how come the diocese expects me to do another degree simply because their guidelines say I should? What a waste of every-one's time. What I need now is on-the-job experience, not a whole lot of box-ticking simply because some bureaucrat at the diocesan office says I must.'

'And that, I'm afraid, is what I mean by disobedience, Rick. Added to that, an unseemly lack of humility. Who on earth do you think you are to expect everyone to duck and weave around your almighty arrogance?!'

'Why? Because if I don't stand up for myself, nobody else will.'

At which point they agreed to end the meeting for a time of prayer and reflection and resume the next afternoon.

Matthew This is one of those situations that has you trying to apportion blame, and I can't decide whose side to take. For instance, I wondered, just as the training incumbent had, where Rick's sense of obedience was, and why he couldn't 'put up and shut up'. It might be considered self-indulgent for a curate to expect a particular calling to receive undue emphasis this early in the process, and all curates have a huge variety of basics to learn. After all, a junior doctor has to learn general medicine before becoming a brain surgeon. So although I found the training incumbent woefully short on interpersonal and communication skills, I understood his point of view and had some sympathy. But then, I thought, the curate's particular aspiration and sense of anointing is precious and should not be diminished or ignored. But that's exactly what I see here, and that caused me to think of it from the curate's point of view.

Beau This is a tricky one and probably another of the dichotomies that we will encounter, because there are indeed two ways of look-ing at this. Let's start with the ideal. A curacy should preferably begin as a blank sheet of paper, because every newly ordained curate is different. Comparisons with previous curates by training incumbents and, especially, by congregations are an unhelpful distraction, while rigid assumptions can set too much in stone too soon. Similarly, it doesn't matter what experience the curate may have had in other areas of life, this is a new beginning and needs to be treated as such. It is often only after the curacy has been going for a while that many curates start to discover the hidden depths of why they are there. The trouble with carefully mapped-out training programmes, working agreements and so on is that for all their benefits, they can sometimes constrict and squeeze a curate out of shape.

Matthew That's all very well, but are you saying that it is inappropriate for a curate to have any sense of the end of the journey?

Beau The life of ministry requires a measured approach to see what shape emerges. If the calling for which the curate feels anointed is genuine, then it will still be there and re-emerge when the time is right. It is equally important, though, to give space for the unexpected to develop and be recognized. Someone pointed out to the architect of a newly built military campus that he had forgotten to include pathways across the lawns. He replied that this was deliberate and said that after the college was opened, they should watch to see where well-worn paths developed as people got used to their accustomed routes from place to place. Only then should proper paths be built to reflect what people did.

Matthew I see, so almost shaping the environment to suit the people, not the other way round.

Beau Precisely.

Matthew But isn't that likely to take it too far in the other direction? After all, Rick had a great deal of experience, and was effectively practising the real ministry to which he felt called; it was obvious that the passion and enthusiasm for his mission was one of the things that made his vocation clear to everyone.

Martyn I think that for more mature and experienced ordinands, perhaps including those who have been readers or who have undertaken other non-ordained ministry, there is a need for a sense check to be taken as to why the person is being ordained. It is perfectly valid for a vocations advisor or a DDO to ask: 'If you are already finding this ministry so fulfilling, what extra dimension are you expecting from being ordained?' For some it may be very easy to respond with conviction – 'Because God has told me to' – but for others the motivation may be harder to discern. That is not to say that Rick shouldn't have been ordained, but it's always a valid question, and is one of the reasons for the selection being so drawn out.

There is nevertheless a sense in which I agree with Beau. Between the training incumbent and the curate, and indeed those involved in the background, there needs to be a sense of seeing which way the journey is going, and keeping that permanently in mind. If the journey has been over-planned, however, then what can happen is that the institution is lulled into a false sense of reality.

In the context of the curacy, this might be translated into two options . . . we let the curacy have its head and go where it will; or else we pre-plan the journey so precisely that there is no wriggle-room at all and the curate is then left with the choice of whether to grin and bear it or to get out. I would always err on the side of protecting the authenticity of the curate's unique gift to the Church. To squeeze that gift into a different shape may give a feeling of progress and permit boxes to be ticked, but is likely to drain that offering of any differentiating value.

Matthew That raises an important issue about how varieties of gifts are perceived in the Church. Many people, including some ordinands, consider the traditional parish setting to be 'proper' ministry, and anything else a self-indulgence or, even worse, second-class priesthood. So when someone like Rick arrives offering his particular gift, one that is decidedly not in mainstream parish ministry, he appears to be demanding one pathway while some in the Church remain resolved to follow the more traditional and more familiar route, because that is where confidence, experience and security appear to reside. And if that includes those who shape training and training incumbents themselves, then we are looking at a self-perpetuating reality firmly based on an old paradigm.

Martyn Yes, that is a risk, and we can certainly take advantage of the mixed economy at theological colleges by doing what has to be done, while encouraging and nurturing ordinands.

Matthew All right. So that deals with the question of a particular vocation. What about this business of being obliged to do an academic degree? Again, the Church of England has its ways of doing things. To quote the 2003 Hind Report:[2] 'It became clear through consultation on the interim report that we have been perceived as being more interested in academic attainment than in the formation of the person for ministry.' While the report goes on to defend itself against that perception, there is a sense that many still promote continuing academic attainment – as opposed to skill-specific training – as central to curacy training, an emphasis that some dioceses embraced with enthusiasm. Whether or not they got it right, isn't learning to accept the requirements of the Church with obedience part of the journey to a fully fruitful life of ministry?

'I'm the humblest priest in the Church'

Martyn Up to a point, yes. But not to the point where the individual loses any sense of freedom or control. After all, especially but not exclusively when they are in a position of responsibility, they will mostly be alone as they take decisions, plan, develop strategies and nearly everything else that they have to do. By that point they have no other framework than canon law and what they have learned during their curacy. A respect for the authority of the Church at a national and diocesan level is one thing: after all, ordination vows are obviously not hollow sentiments pertaining to some artefact of quaint historical ceremony. These vows are solemn, serious, public and personal oaths and undertakings. But that provides little more than a framework. Similarly, the training incumbent has a measure of authority but that doesn't extend to bullying behaviours, nor does it extend to the curate being a doormat to be trampled on.

Beau Can I come in here? You make an important point when you talk about the Church at a national and diocesan level. There is a sense in which there is a sort of postcode lottery about how curacies work. Think of it like this. You have policies laid down by the national Church, generally in the form of guidelines that are not enforceable. How individual dioceses interpret and implement those guidelines is up to them. So we end up with a wide diversity between a Rolls Royce and a Mini . . . over-elaborate training guidelines at one extreme, and cheap and cheerful at the other. Or else prescriptive to the point of squeezing any initiative from the curacy, as opposed to a looseness that leaves everything to the training incumbent and the curate to sort out between them.

So we already have a number of variables, and here is another. Ultimately, the national and local church can do very little to force a training incumbent to follow their guidelines, and little more to force the curate to do so either, except by waving a big stick in the form of withholding a satisfactory end of curacy report.

Matthew So if you take this story as a whole, it seems to be one of somebody being pushed out of shape on several fronts. What is the likely outcome?

Beau That depends hugely. Either they blow their top and go through a very healthy time of pushing the boundaries, which is something we discuss more in the next conversation. Or they repress it, toe the line and continue to be 'good'.

Matthew And which of those would you advocate?

Beau Allow yourself to express the real you, while everyone around you waits patiently for you to sort it out. In my view that is one of the most valuable functions of a curacy.

I must acknowledge, though, that personal resilience and personality have a part to play here as well. Rick took the line that if he didn't stand up for his vision, nobody else would, and he therefore responded robustly. But not everyone is temperamentally made for resistance and rebellion, especially if they have strong tapes playing from their early childhood that 'being good' equals conformity and compliance at all times.

Martyn It shouldn't come to that anyway, because the whole intent of training and formation is to allow people to learn what has to be learned in terms of nuts and bolts (the training bit) and clothing it in the context of who you are, how you tick, the shades of your belief, what you are offering to the Church, thereby finding the right shape for the life of ministry. That's the formation bit. Of course that continues after ordination, but the intent is most definitely to shape and not to pummel. When a curate takes up a title post, there will inevitably be a bit of give and take as everyone involved gets used to each other, but that's the same in any training situation, and happens every time someone new starts working anywhere.

Matthew It sounds good in principle, but for that to work, don't the training incumbent and the rest of the host congregation need to be playing to the same rules? If they have an agenda and will not permit it to be challenged or probed, that will create immediate pressure points. If that pressure becomes unsustainable or too one-sided, then it begins to sound like all-out bullying to me.

Martyn Yes, I used to have a regular procession of former students visiting me to tell me of their woes, and yes, bullying comes up all too frequently.

Matthew But this can't all be about what happened during the curacy or even at theological college. Should we again be looking even further back? We have already explored the possibility of false positives and false negatives at the BAP, and we have also seen that an 80 per cent 'recommended' rate isn't actually all that spectacular given the extensive period of reflection, discernment and assessment even before the candidate reaches a BAP.

Martyn I have to conclude that sometimes candidates go through the entire process and are recommended for training by sheer force of personality rather than true vocation. One sometimes wonders how this can be. By the same token, I am not at all surprised that sometimes a bishop overrules the decision of a BAP. It's inevitable that there will be a margin for error in this, and the Church has to be big enough to work round it, ideally finding the right context and the right form of ministry for each individual who is eventually ordained.

Matthew Is it just about the curates, though? What about the training incumbents?

Martyn There is an issue here which I have already touched on. Many ordinands have a clear vision of a ministry other than in the conventional parish, whether that parish be in the traditional form or part of a large benefice. They may be called to work in chaplaincy or in pioneer ministry, or to serve as a contemplative in the world. They may be offering their vocation on a part-time basis as they fulfil a parallel secular career. They may have all sorts of gifts that don't seem to fit. The Church of England believes that all ordained ministry needs to begin by being grounded in some kind of parish context. It believes that ministry is further tested, refined and developed in the fundamental grounding of serving people, in the midst of a major part of their everyday existence and experiences. Namely, the context we know as 'the parish'. Thus, regardless of the eventual context of their ministry, it is to a 'conventional' parish priest that they are apprenticed. In a sense, therefore, it doesn't matter what tweaks the Church makes to IME4–7 and other aspects of ongoing training and formation, because the context remains pretty rigid.

Beau Developing that further, Martyn, one of my great concerns is that people are the product of their own journey: curates and training incumbents are no exception. In psychological terms, the curacy is a parental relationship, and if the curate (the child) has only one view of a training incumbent (the parent), there is a risk that the curate may adopt that model should he or she becomes a training incumbent in the future. After all, look at little children mimicking their parents as they sternly tell off a younger sibling. But, of course, curates aren't children and if it was a bad experience because, to be blunt, it was badly done, then they may equally use that as a template for how *not* to be a training incumbent.

Matthew Yes, I suspect we have all responded to bosses in that way at one time or another, but I do wonder about the force of expectations and role models here. Amanda Bloor's research following a number of clergy through their journeys to a life of ministry is interesting:

> When ordinands talked about their initial stirrings of vocation, they often mentioned clergy whose example had inspired them to consider if they too might be called by God . . . The individuals they had observed became templates of what dedicating oneself to Christian service could involve . . . Yet if these 'ideal' images are not developed into more fully rounded models, ordinands are primed for discordance between what they believe and what they experience.[3]

This looks remarkably like the influence we all carry into adult life and often model, be it parents, school teachers or first bosses.

It's a natural way of being. I suppose the alarm bell rings when it turns out that the training incumbent doesn't, after all, conform to the role model. And that reminds me of a recurring complaint. Several curates have suggested that training incumbents *ought* to have emotional intelligence and *ought* to be people with qualifications in adult education. Actually, whether it's from the pulpit or anywhere else, I am never comfortable with assertions that include 'ought' or 'should'. That notwithstanding, how do you see it?

'Spoiled for choice, really'

Martyn Yes, of course it would be helpful for training incumbents to be people with all-round intellectual, emotional and spiritual intelligence. Actually, even though that expectation may not be an explicit dimension of selection assessment, I am sure that it must be there implicitly.

Beau I agree at one level, but I too am uncomfortable when people take a moral high ground and point everywhere but at themselves. Yes, as Martyn says, it would be nice. But isn't it reasonable to ask, very gently, whether the people who become so indignant about this might want to take a look at their own emotional intelligence? The phrase 'Physician, heal thyself' comes to mind.

Martyn And as for the adult education qualification, yes, I can see the point, especially with the current form of IME4–7. It might indeed be an advantage, but so might all sorts of other skills that clergy may have acquired along the way before entering ministry. If we try to prescribe the ideal mix for the perfect training incumbent, we would probably never have sufficient. The reality is that the Church must find the best people for the job, and if curates expect them to be perfect in every respect they are in for a disappointment.

Beau And that's a positive thing, Martyn, another dichotomy. Yes, it would be nice for curates if training incumbents were perfectly integrated people and were qualified in every relevant area. But the reality is that the curate is likely to learn a great deal more about how to relate to different people if the training incumbent is *not* perfect. And if it comes to a head in a conflict of views, fine: it usually comes out right in the end. That's what we call professional adolescence, but we'll come to that later.

Martyn As for expectations in general, in the same way that Amanda Bloor points to misconceptions and clouded vision as a potentially distorted view of the reality of the life of ministry, so a very bad experience of a curacy can have devastating knock-on effects years down the road. While I agree that short-term disagreements and difficulties may provide a good opportunity to fine-tune the relationship between the curate and the training incumbent, I am equally certain that that should not be seen as an excuse for dismissing the very real concerns of some curates. That is one thing that makes the Ministry Division initiative about training incumbents so important. The evidence for its success will be not in how it is communicated to and by dioceses, though, but how it is actually implemented and managed, and what happens in the reality of the curacy relationship. And in the specific case you mention, Matthew, the training incumbent needs to realize that virtually any incoming curate will inevitably have preconceptions. These need to be gently acknowledged and explored, as areas for fertile discussion, not as the basis for hostilities.

Matthew So, to summarize, we have a paradox. Yes, it is appropriate to have a framework to help guide the curate and the training incumbent through the curacy, and that framework needs to have a didactic side to it; but there is an equal need for flexibility to nurture vocations and to ensure that the God-given gift is used to the full.

Beau I might express it even more bluntly. In order for the square peg to thrive in a square hole, it has to be capable of surviving in a round hole too, provided that excessive force is not used to achieve that!

Matthew So assertive behaviour is fine, but bullying is not?

Beau Correct. Yes, and that rubs both ways, but we'll get into that later.

Points for reflection

Curates

- To what eventual ministry do you feel called, and to what extent are you open to further stirrings of the Holy Spirit to change?
- How do you balance the need to be yourself and the need to 'fit in'?
- What image do you have of the 'ideal priest', and how ready are you to forgive your training incumbent for not being that person?

Training incumbents

- How do you establish the balance between a curate's clear calling to a particular sort of ministry and getting the basics done?
- Do you know the difference between assertiveness and bullying?
- When you sense the curate's expectations of you and sense that you may be falling short, with whom do you discuss it?

Dioceses

- How flexible is your interpretation of the requirements of IME4–7, and to what extent do you implement guidelines from the national Church?
- Given your resource constraints, how do you ensure that a 'one-size-fits-all' approach is not enshrined into IME4–7, whether in terms of the content or its curacies?
- What training and guidance do you give on how to conduct performance reviews and appraisals?

3

Same old, same old

————◆•●•◆————

We have seen that today's curacies are taking place in a changing world with conscious attempts to improve the pathway to the life of ministry for all involved. We will never achieve perfection, which might suggest that the remainder of this book will be purely about curacies that fail. But what do we mean by failure? The reality is that the vast majority of curates, even those who have to endure choppy waters, usually emerge safe and sound into the next stage of their ordained ministry. This story, of Christopher, Angela and their family, is an example of just such an unremarkable curacy.

It was about three months into Christopher's post-curacy position as assistant priest in a rural team ministry. It was the end of the day, and as usual he and his wife were both exhausted, but feeling fulfilled; the children were in bed, and Christopher and Angela were reflecting with pleasure on their journey together.

They had been friends since childhood. They'd gone to the same school, and had been in Sunday school together. They were both active in church life, went to Bible studies together and rarely missed a home group. As they grew through their teen years they became active in other ways, and eventually he became assistant to the youth worker. For her part, Angela joined the Sunday school leadership team. At college they were both prominent in the Scripture Union, and nobody was surprised when they became engaged; nor was the vicar surprised when Christopher confided in him that he felt a very strong call to ordained ministry.

They were married in the summer before he started at theological college, and the parish gave them a good send-off, promising continued prayer support. The vicar had helped him to select a theological college where he would feel comfortable, and which would affirm Angela's ministry as a clergy wife. They both sailed through the three years and were fortunate when the college and diocese were able to find him a title post where his lifelong experience of this sort of churchmanship would be allowed to blossom further.

By the time he started at Christ Church, their son Timothy was 18 months old and Angela was expecting again. The parish helped them with generosity as they settled into the curate's house that had been rented for them, and they were soon busily involved. Having been brought up with a strong focus on the Word, they had feared that they might be obliged to change. It was a relief to find that here, too, the focus was on the Bible fair and square. To his delight, Christopher discovered that he would not be required to wear vestments except for certain occasions, and the model of leadership that he and Angela found was what they had always been used to.

The three years of the curacy flew by. Because he had fitted in so well, and always accepted without question the decisions and methods of the vicar and the rest of the leadership team, there had been few disputes. Angela was centrally involved in forming the new Mothers and Toddlers group, and until the third baby came along, she taught in Sunday school. Christopher worked on the street mission and at the plant daughter church, and although they were sad not to spend more time together, they both felt a strong sense of fulfilment in their joint ministry.

By the end of the curacy, Christopher's credentials were impressive and it didn't take him long to find a position as assistant priest in a lively team ministry covering several rural parishes. It had all seemed so seamless, and they wondered why some of the other people they knew had gone through such difficulties. Why, only the other day they had heard about Teresa, whom they'd known at college, who had had to be moved to another church because of problems in her curacy.

Christopher and Angela shook their heads sadly, muttering a knowledgeable comment about sacrifice and obedience. After a pause, they opened their Bibles and said their bedtime prayers.

Matthew It sounds idyllic. In fact, when I read of Christopher and Angela, I was reminded of Mr Bennet's observation:[1] 'You are each of you so complying, that nothing will ever be resolved on.' Nothing could be better, so I don't see why we have even included this example, except perhaps to represent the many curacies that prosper. So why are you shaking your head, Beau?

Beau Because a curacy is a priestly adolescence. This adolescence is part dependency, part bolshiness, in checking the boundaries in a way in which that particular curate can determine how to become a priest in their own particular way, through trial and error.

Matthew But surely obedience lies at the heart of priestly ministry, especially in the early days?

Beau To become proficient, one must succeed in continually practising a particular skill; to learn something one must fail. If you don't fail, you don't try to discover a different way of doing things. A failure may be defined as a 'different way of doing things from the right way'. Exploring how these two elements combine, we use the analogy of a professional adolescence for a priest in training.

Matthew But surely some people just get it right? What's wrong with that?

Beau There are a lot of hoops to go through to be a priest. Essentially checks are made to see that the curate is a 'good' boy or girl, in that he or she conforms to particular norms. This demonstration of conformity to a norm continues through theological college on an academic level, on a moral level, and in being able to learn new skills.

Matthew Surely nobody could have been more of a 'good boy' than Christopher in that example?

Beau Let me put it like this. The term 'sky pilot' has been used to describe clergy. Now, in order to get a regular pilot's licence you have to intentionally put your plane into a downward spin and pull out of it. In the same way, priests have to deal creatively and to respond well when things go wrong and to become used to disappointing people's expectations without alienating them excessively, while widening their thinking.

Essentially this also has to be practised with their training incumbents. It's a skill to be able to bypass a determined authority figure to do things the way you honestly feel they should be done, while going along with them on another level. Therefore there is an opportunity in curacy to practise this skill.

Matthew So you are saying that because Christopher toed the line, never rebelled, and always seemed to get it right, he missed the opportunity to learn from failure?

Beau Yes. A clergy person has to become a priest in a way that matches his or her individuality, otherwise they might be tempted to 'role-play' a priest in an unconvincing way. This is not as far-fetched as it sounds.

Having taught theological students to enable them to learn how to deal with difficulties, one particular student absolutely refused to engage in any role-play whatsoever during the entire training. Many years later, after that person became an incumbent, there was a lot of difficulty in that priest's parish. I happened to be visiting someone there and went along to the Eucharist, which the incumbent was celebrating. I was struck during the service that something was quite wrong, and it took me a long time to put my finger on just what it was. Even though the priest was properly ordained and had been a priest for some time, essentially he came across as a layperson pretending to be a priest by doing an imitation of what a layperson thought a priest might do. In short, to keep the 'magic' of being a priest alive, he had not allowed theological training to inform or to alter his thinking in any way and dilute that lay image of what a priest was supposed to be.

Matthew But surely one of the main formational purposes of theological college was to teach him to empty himself of 'me' and simply to do as they said?

Beau Well, if they did, they missed a trick. He came across as inauthentic, not engaging with individuals at all, in terms of listening, empathy or dialogue. He had managed to get through the system while remaining essentially a pre-trained lay person. Christopher sounds the same. He comes across as exactly the same person as when he was helping out at Sunday school.

Matthew Yes, but Christopher got on well with everyone. That was what everybody liked about him. And nothing ever went 'wrong', as you put it. So how might it go if it works well?

Beau Essentially the curate can use his or her personhood to be of service to others. Incarnation means to get involved very personally with a humble but trained identification with others, first to identify and then to walk alongside them towards a better and fuller state. It uses genuine humanity as a way of revealing the transcendent within the ordinary. In this transformation, the image has to 'fail' so that the humanity can get through. If the image doesn't fail, it is narcissism.

Alexander Lowen identifies the presence of narcissism[2] as being identifiable by the person having a 'wooden face'. It is visible in some actors and pop stars, with the wooden smile, the frozen expression – frozen in the way they look the best. Unfortunately, it can also be fatal.

If you put a paving slab on the grass, it kills the grass beneath it. If you put on a rigid, contrived mask of perfection for a long time, it can block out the personality beneath it; this is one reason why narcissistic people tend to exhibit suicidal behaviour. When they realize that life isn't perfect after all, they cannot deal with it. The personality has been killed by the mask.

The clergyperson can wear such a mask, which not only blocks human contact and the ability to empathize, but can also lead indirectly to suicidal or professional self-destructive behaviour. A person can get trapped in role-playing a priest and think that this is his or her authentic self. This doesn't work indefinitely: the priest can wear a false mask for too long, becoming the 'perfect priest', then sometimes, quite dramatically, the illusion of perfection can be removed – the priest might be caught with a hand in the till or some equally startling action. While it is shocking to all concerned, it might end up being both destructive and liberating, with the priest trying to become more genuine.

Matthew You make it sound very dramatic. But this feels a million miles away from where Christopher is. Everyone liked how genuine he seemed: certainly no masks there.

Beau I don't agree. And that is why being taught how to use vulnerability and human failing in the service of others is so very important. Basically, discovering the 'transparent self' can be learned in curacy, where you can be pleasant and professional on the outside, without disguising from the other how you really feel inside. Christopher's situation is especially interesting because it dates right back to childhood.

It is interesting to look at this professional training relationship as paralleling the relationship between parents and children in terms of stages. In the first part of life, the parents nurture and parent the child. They make the rules, the child obeys. Then in adolescence, children rebel against the rules in order to become more fully themselves: rebelling, while at the same time also needing the rules and boundaries to be there to push against for definition of self. It's a love–hate relationship. The end of adolescence is when the children, while continuing to develop, no longer need to rebel to define themselves 'against' everything.

Matthew We all know how messy adolescence can be and how much parents have to endure when a teenager goes into yet another moody sulk. So how should the training incumbent behave and react while the curate is experimenting to see how far the boundaries can be pushed?

Martyn Speaking from my own experience, my curacy was liberated by the attitude of my training incumbent. He said that when I got things wrong, or if congregation members came to him and complained about something I had done during my curacy, he would take full responsibility; and that he would give me full credit for all the good things I did. That gave me the confidence I needed.

Beau That's fine, but for every incumbent like that there may be others who lose their rag, and that's where things go wrong. In supervision, guilt is collected by the counsellor (or by the incumbent from the parishioner via the curate) who processes it like a laundry, understands it and takes the sting out of it. The incumbent, therefore, holds bad feelings as supervisor. In all supervision, whether for therapy or in the Church, if the supervisor (incumbent) loses his or her cool and shouts at the patient (curate) it is amplified by the power of three and the effect is absolutely devastating. For this reason, no matter what I feel strongly as a therapeutic supervisor, I try never to express anger of my own; if I do, it is a mess I have to clean up afterwards in terms of putting the counsellor (priest) back together again. Most of the mistakes I have made as a supervisor have been to let slip feelings of condemnation, even moderate ones. It is a pity that incumbents in their supervisory capacity are never taught this; there is damage to put right whenever it happens, sometimes long-lasting, and often involving the pastoral care advisor.

Matthew Yes, I see. We have already discussed that more is being done to provide greater rigour around the selection and training of training incumbents, although we have also seen that guidelines guarantee nothing unless they are implemented. For the time being, though, let's stick with professional adolescence. What happens next?

'Both God and I are disappointed in you!'

Beau Although the parent–child relationship remains, they are now more like brothers and sisters to each other. It's ideally a non-bossy support of equals: the parents cannot so easily tell the children what to do, but, if needed, are there for them.

Then, later in life, when the parents get old and frail, the roles are reversed as the children parent their own parents. This is a time of realization: as the children adopt the parenting role for their own parents, they are often doing so in the way they saw modelled by their parents.

Matthew Yes, I understand that, and to an extent it sounds a bit like the journey from parent–child to adult–adult in transactional analysis, but what on earth has it got to do with a curacy?

Beau Stay with me! In the training of paratroopers, they reach a stage where they fold their own parachutes, rather than having them folded for them. If they have made a mistake and have not done it exactly right, they are the first to know about it – though, of course, they have a back-up.

Similarly parents have trained their children in parenting them and so they have folded their own parenting parachute. If they have been dictatorial, the children are likely to be dictatorial back to them in old age. At some point the incumbent may be in need, and the curate then 'parents their parent' in the way he or she has been taught. This can happen in a curacy when the two switch roles on occasion.

Also, in terms of becoming an incumbent, the curate has to be able to take a stand in a diplomatic way; otherwise, if a curate hasn't learned to disagree properly and effectively, he or she is not ready to become an incumbent. This learning is reflected in the changing relationship between incumbent and curate, which becomes more equal than when it first began. By this stage, in an ideal world, we may wonder, a bit like the characters of Jeeves and Wooster, who is really in charge in the relationship!

Matthew OK. In this case, they were more like colleagues than boss and subordinate. But there was a natural pecking order. They both knew it and complied. The way you put it makes it sound as if Christopher's golden journey is just an explosion waiting to happen.

Beau Exactly! And to make matters worse, picking up on your earlier reference to *Pride and Prejudice*, if Christopher and Angela are really quite so very compliant, never argue about anything, and that never resolves, then it may be another explosion waiting to happen. So you see, it isn't just about the curate, or about the curate and the training incumbent: everyone is liable to be affected in a curacy that does not go through professional adolescence.

There is another factor here, which is worth mentioning. It comes from the psychoanalyst Wilfred Bion,[3] who said that basically there are two types of groups that people form. One is a 'basic assumptions group', which relies on everyone believing the same thing. Alcoholics Anonymous is such a group: its 12-step programme is something to which everyone adheres. It's a strength in that everyone holds the same principle and no one disagrees. If it operates well and everyone complies the experience will be quite smooth and uplifting. However, if you disagree with the commonly held principles of the group, you feel the wall of the whole group being against you and it is very overpowering.

The other type of group is a 'work group' (or therapy group), in which individuals discover their distinctive roles by taking slightly different positions. Here you find your identity by taking a stand, finding support in a sub-group, defining yourself and your position by argument and dialogue. Identity is built, defined and refined through support, dialogue and robust disagreement.

My hunch is that Christopher found a nice place in a church where everyone agreed. It is lovely and warm where everyone thinks the same. So what's the problem? In the psychiatric hospital where I worked, several people were admitted who had initially found warm support in a church house group, but things turned against them when they disagreed with powerful individuals. Their feeling that 'the whole Church had turned against them' was so devastating that they had to spend time in hospital.

Both groups work in their own way: one by conformity, which is a unifying feeling, the other by disagreement and redefinition. My hunch is that the latter is more robust in that the Church often thrives best under pressure. And that at some point, as Jesus pointed out, you have to expect persecution, so be ready for it. The key thing here is that if you don't encounter strong disagreement in your curacy and deal with it then, you won't be prepared when it inevitably comes later on.

Matthew So if you are saying that a curacy that does not go through professional adolescence in some form is missing something, what would be your message to the Christophers of this world?

Martyn Going back to first principles, I would urge every ordinand to choose a college or course that will challenge their preconceptions. Studying at a 'safe' college may seem the obvious thing to do, but it is likely to make for a very one-dimensional life of ministry. Similarly, I would take full advantage of placements during training, to challenge expectations and offer new perspectives. And I would certainly say the same about the choice of title post. In this example, I think that Christopher was badly advised, since he was not really being offered a genuine learning opportunity. I heard of a bishop who 'recommended' that a very Anglo-Catholic ordinand accept a title post which resulted in being paired with a Conservative Evangelical training incumbent. Neither had experience of the other's perspective, so I can see what he was trying to do. It certainly added colour to the curate's otherwise rather monochrome experience, and perhaps at the same time shook up what can be an almost self-congratulatory 'we do what we do rather well' culture in the host church. I'm not sure I would go quite that far, but the principle still applies.

Matthew I am still slightly puzzled as to why someone like Christopher, with such a clear pedigree, should have their curacy branded as, at the least, sub-optimal. Why can't he simply stick with that specialization?

Martyn Perhaps I can help. The answer may lie in Fowler's concept of 'stages of faith',[4] which run all the way from rigid literalism to open-mindedness, seeing value in all faiths and shades of faith. The reality is that the life of ministry, especially in parish life where there are people of all faiths and none, is of necessity going to require a sense of value in all things, and the ability and confidence to 'live their lives to the full in service of others without any real worries or doubts'. The problem for Christopher is that he has experienced only one shade of faith, which has become so ingrained in him that it feels like the one and only version of the truth, and it has become something to which he has learned to comply without questioning. In the absence of challenge or the opportunity to observe and experience other shades of faith, that rigid literalism is liable to become ever more rigid. It could be argued that someone who has had such an easy passage has actually made little progress on Fowler's continuum and may, in M. Scott Peck's words,[5] 'become attached to the forms of their religion and get extremely upset when these are called into question'. If it hasn't already happened, the curacy represents perhaps the last opportunity to progress the curate to a more rounded view of life.

Matthew Yes, and that whole theme of questioning and pushing the boundaries brings us back to relationships in a church setting. Gerard Hughes[6] writes of our infant, adolescent and adult phases and that reminds me of a friend who was asked to leave a church because he kept asking inconvenient questions. He was obviously going through his adolescent phase and it was more convenient for the church for everybody to remain as dependent infants, consuming the spiritual food delivered by the leadership team without adulteration or discussion. If that's bad for the congregation, how much worse must it be if the priest is also stuck in that 'infant' state? Are we saying that that is Christopher's fundamental problem? And not just his, because it sounds as if his sending church, his theological college and his title post have colluded to keep him in that state. No wonder you think his curacy has fallen short.

Martyn Yes, that puts it very well. Actually, one might ask why this was not picked up at Christopher's BAP. I have certainly heard of cases where an applicant very similar to Christopher was asked to gain some experience in a very different church, and then return to the BAP at a later date. That gave the opportunity to assess whether the applicant was temperamentally capable of seeing and living different expressions of faith, and I would advise that in all similar cases.

Matthew That seems to make complete sense to me. I do recall, Beau, that when I told you about a particular curacy that was going wrong, I was astonished when you said, 'Oh, good!' I know that you were not looking for misery or failure for the sake of it, so as we approach the end of this discussion of a so-called perfect curacy that wasn't, what were you really trying to say?

Beau Quite simply: no curacy is complete without professional adolescence. When I completed my own curacy, a wise old priest asked me how it had gone. I replied that it had been uneventful and that there had been no major issues. The priest replied, 'Oh, I *am* sorry!' It's counter-intuitive, I know. Of course, we all hope that in most cases challenges will be met and ideas will be modified without undue strain, but unless there comes the point where the curate boils over with frustration and reacts strongly, whether verbally, emotionally or even physically, then it seems extremely unlikely that the curacy has done its job.

Matthew So that is another paradox: a curacy that appears to be a success may be a failure.

Points for reflection

Curates

- How much do you expect your preconceptions to be challenged, and are you open to that, even looking for it?

- Are you someone who looks for the 'safe' options when it comes to looking for a theological institution and a title post, and what are your expectations at the end?
- If you lose your temper with the training incumbent, will you view that as failure or a growth opportunity?

Training incumbents

- How comfortable are you with the idea of professional adolescence?
- How challenging are you in selecting curates?
- What do you see as the purpose of a curacy from your church's point of view?

Dioceses

- How involved do you get in helping to ensure that the right curates get the right growth opportunities in their curacies?
- How would you characterize a successful curacy – and a troubled curacy?
- One bishop was heard to say to a group of newly ordained curates, 'Make sure you don't give me any problems!' Is that another way of saying that curates should be seen and not heard, and do you subscribe to it?

4

One of the gang

———•◦•———

Arriving as a curate in a new parish for the first time must be rather like being a new teacher at the beginning of term at school. Everyone is looking at you, wondering who you are and what you will be like. How will you adapt to their culture? If you are married, what's your family like? You are likely to arrive knowing nobody other than the incumbent, and it may be in a part of the country you are not familiar with. Your theology may be challenged from day one by different ways of doing things. All the while, you and any family are probably going through the upheaval of moving house. Taken together, this represents a major challenge so soon after leaving the relatively safe world of theological training, whatever form that has taken, and it may rapidly feel like a comedown after the euphoria of ordination.

Many churches will make every effort to ensure that you and your family feel welcome. Some, especially those that think of themselves as 'training congregations', take great pride in how they care for their curates. People may arrive on the doorstep on moving-in day bearing casseroles, apple pies, bottles of wine, bunches of flowers and more besides. In some congregations, they may even have been in before you arrived, decorating and cleaning so that everything is ready for you.

Conversely, others will understand that you need time to settle in; they will make it known that they are there for you if needed, but will otherwise leave you alone. After all, it takes a while to sort out boxes and crates, get connected to broadband, locate the kettle, learn how the heating works, and find out why there's that funny smell in the larder.

Sadly, though, some incoming curates simply feel neglected and ignored, as if they were not there at all. They may arrive and find nothing to indicate that anyone was expecting them other than a pile of papers and rotas on the kitchen table.

The way you are accepted into the community may be a reflection of how the particular church understands the purpose of a curacy. A new member to be welcomed into the church family? A potential blessing to the church? A spare pair of hands? A learning opportunity? A chance for some fresh air? A resource to be used and exploited?

Let's hear how Tom handled all this when he and his wife Samantha and their three children moved in.

Tom was a gregarious sort of person, and when he started his curacy he was determined to get to know people and establish himself with them as quickly as possible. His previous life in business had taught him to be something of a chameleon, meeting people at their own levels. This had made him a popular manager and successful in his job. Despite his seniority, he had always taken his turn going to get the coffee for everyone, and he never missed the opportunity to go to the pub with them all on Friday nights. This made for a good working relationship all round.

Now he had arrived at St Mary's, he felt that he could usefully take the same approach. He explained this in his first sermon, and was warmly greeted by congregation members afterwards. Later that week, meeting the Mothers' Union for the first time, he encouraged them all to address him as Tom. Every Saturday at Men's Breakfast, he joked and bantered with those present, making sure that he would be seen as a friend and that it was safe to say anything with him around. Some of the things that were said were not doctrinally accurate and some were downright heresy, but it didn't seem to bother him; he listened and smiled. He sat on the floor in jeans and T-shirt with the children at Sunday school and encouraged them, too, to call him Tom.

Samantha played her part too. She had open house for all the young mums, and made it clear that she and Tom wanted simply to be part of the church family, not set apart in some way. Tom reflected this by wearing an open-necked shirt most of the time, only rarely his collar.

All went well for some months, during which time he established some very close relationships.

The first sign that something was not quite right was when one of the men stopped coming to Men's Breakfast. He hadn't sent any message, but simply stopped coming. Tom discussed it with his training incumbent, and sensed that instead of the warm, easy dialogue that they had previously enjoyed, there was now a reserved coolness in the air. Actually, he had already noticed at their monthly supervision meetings that the incumbent was becoming a little distant.

At their initial meeting, right at the start of the curacy, the incumbent had said, 'I want us to be best friends.' Tom had taken this generous gesture at face value. He had been friendly, enjoyed their lunches with their families at the vicarage table, and their chats about their shared interest in premiership football. But now something was wrong.

'I'm sorry to say this, Tom,' his incumbent explained, 'but the reason that Jeff has stopped coming to Men's Breakfast is that he feels he cannot trust himself to be in the same room with you while he is sorting through some personal issues. He has been coming to me instead. When he first asked for some of my time, I suggested that he have a chat with you, since you were getting on so well, and I thought it would be a good learning opportunity for you. It didn't take long to discover that what he actually needed was someone who was more detached, who could be non-judgemental and provide objective feedback.

> He said that some of the banter had revealed things about you that would make it very difficult to talk at the very deep and personal level that was now needed.'
>
> Tom was distraught. His approach had been intended to make it possible for people to feel comfortable with him, and now he was being told that this approach had achieved the very opposite effect. It wasn't just the vicar who had noticed. He sometimes had a feeling that certain parishioners were laughing *at* him, not *with* him, and that the friendly relationships he thought he had established were beginning to wear a bit thin.
>
> All he had tried to do was to make friends.

Matthew What on earth went wrong? This sounds like a good, integrated person using his experience and his interpersonal skills to very good effect, rapidly building up the sort of relationships that are so important within a curacy. And how brilliant that the incumbent established a friendly working relationship at the outset. Please enlighten me.

Martyn I hardly know where to start, and I see Beau straining at the leash as well. If there's one thing I hear more than any other, it is stories of curates who overcompensate for the fact that they are new and don't know anybody, by trying to be 'one of the lads', to coin a phrase. They seem to want to be friends with everyone, to be involved in everything. I'm sorry: it's asking for trouble.

Matthew So what's the problem?

Martyn It's not one problem, it's many. For a start, a priest cannot be 'an ordinary member of the congregation'. The point of ordination is that one is set apart for ministry. That does not mean detached, incidentally, because ministry is always embedded in a context – it could not be ministry, otherwise. But ordination does set the minister apart from the congregation. That is what the congregation normally *require*, in terms of symbolic roles, ritual, teaching and pastoral functions. Indeed, not only does the congregation require this; so does God. So, let's start with what I think is the fundamental issue.

Priests are not actually a species apart, granted,[1] but they are supposed to be different – and so represent and embody that difference *within* their congregations and parishes. The whole process of discernment is about discovering whether the vocation is a general one to serve, or specifically a call to priesthood. There are, of course, different views of what that means, but the moment of ordination is liminal; it is a doorway into a new way of life and, for some, a new state of being.

However you see it, a priest is one who serves: that is what the word 'deacon' means. Priests and bishops are deacons too, and it is that fundamental and sacrificial life of service that sets the clergy apart within a congregation.

Beau Perhaps I could put what Martyn says in relational terms. I think the best example of the dichotomy the priest faces is wrapped up in the word that some people use to address them – 'Father'; similarly (perhaps fewer) female priests are sometimes addressed as 'Mother'. In the family, the parent, whether father or mother, has a particular role, which appears contradictory, but is more paradoxical. The parent has to be both an authority figure and a kindly parent at the same time. The parent is a friend to the children and to the family, but always has to maintain the role of being 'above' as well, in order for the family to feel safe by being cared for – that someone is in charge. Frequently the person in the parent role has to be slightly 'above the conflict' while at the same time understanding and remaining involved on a human level. So the parent is friendly and approachable, but simultaneously needs to be slightly distant.

Individuals can thrive if the hierarchy gives them good parenting. It makes us feel safe to know that we are parented. For example, when Pope John XXIII was elected pope and his first serious issue was presented to him to resolve, he replied, 'This is very serious;

I shall have to take this up with the Pope. Goodness, I can't do this any more because I *am* the Pope! In that case, I shall have to take it up with God.' In short, even the person who is 'top parent' still needs to be parented in some way from above. The priest cannot relinquish that role in being chummy.

Matthew I see. But that doesn't stop them being friends, does it?

Martyn Friendly, yes, but friends? Clergy need to be discerning here. I could certainly *not* countenance a 'friendly to all but friends with none' approach. We have experienced strong friendships that have grown and developed within the parishes we have served in. And those friendships remain strong and important for us today. But we need to be mindful that some in the congregation may be jealous of such a relationship, where it develops. But that on its own is *not* an argument for having no friends in the parish. It is merely a 'note to self': be mindful of the dynamic, and attend to the boundaries and borders as needed.

Moreover, some parishioners may interpret the general friendliness of clergy – a good, holy and godly characteristic of ministers to cultivate into a virtue – as an invitation to an actual specific

'I wonder if this new T-shirt will make me more approachable?'

friendship, which cannot always be reciprocated. Apart from anything else, real friendships take time to develop. And I have not
noticed many clergy these days who are 'time-rich', with lots of
space in their diaries, with time on their hands for making new
friends. Seeing your old ones can be hard enough.

But let's put that question to one side as I explore several of the
things that are central to a priest's work, activities and states of
mind that set the clergy apart. I'm not talking about the liturgical
activities, though they are important. I'm talking more about relational things. Let's start with authority.

Priests, especially those in parish ministry, have authority in
the sense that they are the ones with the full range of theological
training and priestly formation. The Church expects them to be
guardians of orthodox thinking, and congregations expect them
to know the answers to their questions. At a practical level, think
of a Bible study where several interpretations are being aired.
If one of those interpretations is plain wrong, it is the priest's
duty to at least challenge that, and quite likely to put forward a
different perspective. Part of a curate's on-the-job experience is
about developing ways of doing this in ways that help people
in a positive way without discouraging them. In Tom's case, he
was trying to participate in Bible studies as an equal; he was
effectively surrendering the authority that is built into his job –
something that, in the end, congregations expect of their priest.
And that applies as much to the curate as to the incumbent.

Another dimension of the priestly life is about the confidences
that people may share with the clergy. In Tom's situation, any one
of the men or women he is being a pal to today may tomorrow
come to him to share, offload, weep or confess. This is something
the priest has to get used to, and it is made all the more difficult
if it suddenly becomes awkward to meet that same person in other
settings – at services, house groups, at the shops and so on. How
can the priest adopt the sort of detachment required in such
situations if formality and role-recognition have been removed in
previous exchanges and in other settings?

So to come back to your question: yes, of course there must be some sort of warmth and a friendly demeanour, but that is very different from creating friendships that by definition remove the very boundaries that enable a priest to be true to the calling.

Matthew But many jobs require you to be able to keep confidences, whether on business matters or personal things. For instance, from my time in industry I can remember knowing well in advance about a business reorganization that was going to involve a number of redundancies. I had to be able to work normally with those people until the moment was right for the announcements. That came with the job. I really don't see why that is so different for a priest.

Martyn Yes, to an extent you are right, but church life presents a particular challenge. In your business life, how often did you bump into the families of those co-workers, or meet them socially, or associate with them at events where the co-worker and their entire families were present? Let me spell it out. If someone comes to see me on a delicate pastoral matter that is particular and personal to that individual, I should not assume, if I meet their spouse or partner casually, a little later in the day, that the knowledge I gained earlier will be known by this other person, or has been shared.

If the nature of the curate's everyday relationships is as casual as Tom and many others try to make it, how can any sense of objectivity be maintained when such problems arise? There must be an ability to maintain relational and spiritual objectivity.

There's another dimension to this. In most working environments, you are insulated to an extent by hierarchies, role relationships and other aspects of the structure. It is only your position and, yes, your status as a priest that provides that sort of insulation between you and congregation members.

Matthew That makes it sound a rather lonely job, just at the time when the curate and family have been torn away from the theological college community or their home environment, are taking on new roles and really need friends.

Martyn Yes, that is true, and I'm afraid it comes with the job. That is why it is so important for the curate to have as wide a support network as possible, and why it is essential for that network to include people outside the parish, chaplaincy or other place of work. Spiritual directors, ministry development groups, long-lasting prayer triangles from college days, and old friends from a previous life, however far away they may live . . . they are the people with whom the curate can pour it all out on an equal basis, not parishioners. That is a reason why clergy spouse support activities are so important, and why many dioceses are proactive in making them happen.

Beau Thanks for that prompt about family life, Martyn. There's another dimension that we mustn't forget. Any sense of relational ambiguity, especially early in the life of ministry, has the potential to result in disaster for everyone involved. I don't think I need to spell it out, except to say that once relationships have become over-friendly, then it can be an incredibly short journey in some circumstances from a wholesome interaction to the sort of thing the gutter press in all their prurient pomp love to expose. What sort of things? That's the trouble: often at the time they may seem relatively harmless. It might be a second glass of wine on a home visit, for instance, or a counselling session in a bedroom because there is nowhere else to be alone, or a hug that lingers too long in a confused response to the high emotion that can be aroused at intense spiritual events. Of course, it rarely gets to be quite that serious, but that's purely a question of degree: however far it goes, the basis for avoiding problems must be to set ordinary day-to-day relationships at appropriate levels and to learn to establish boundaries from the outset.[2]

Martyn Actually this is something that requires attention before the curacy even begins: in the selection process for new ordinands, in the selection of training incumbents, and in the allocation of ordinands to their title posts. I remember a case where I had to intervene when a prospective training incumbent made inappropriate, so-called man-to-man comments to me about a female ordinand who was about to become his curate. It was clear that the curacy could not be allowed to proceed and I was able to ensure that the curate was given a different title post and that the priest concerned was not permitted to be a training incumbent in the future. This again underlines the importance of ensuring that only the right people are chosen to be training incumbents, and then that the right curates are placed with the right training incumbents.

'It's simple, really. All you have to do is keep parishioners at arm's length and you'll be fine'

Of course, this is not just about training incumbents, and I would hope that the sequence of discernment, selection and training of prospective ordinands would give sufficient opportunities for the Church to observe and act appropriately. This is more easily said than done: the criteria for selection of prospective ordinands include one on Personality and Character and another on Relationships, but neither of them explicitly goes into the reality of what can happen if the sexual chemistry with a colleague or a member of the congregation takes a wrong turn. And, as you say, Beau, the beginning of sexual misbehaviour can be very subtle. Fortunately, the people involved generally see the signs and stand back, sometimes seeking a break in the working relationship, or else putting the curacy on a new footing that removes or minimizes the risks. The trouble is that sometimes the people involved see the truth of the destructive course they have taken only when they realize they are already on a slippery slope from which there is little chance of rescue. The Church is sometimes accused of being obsessed with sex, but we are right to take it seriously because when it is misused the damage that can be caused is incalculable; thereafter it can be very difficult for the grace of God to be let back into what can seem an unredeemable situation.

Matthew I'm not sure that all ordained clergy would see it in quite such dark terms as that, but let's move on.

Martyn Sorry, but there's more. In purely relational terms, it may seem trivial compared with what Beau was just talking about, but all sorts of snags can arise if the curate, or any priest for that matter, becomes too matey with congregation members. There can be a blurring of roles. Who am I talking to today? The preacher? My friend? My drinking partner? My confessor? My teacher? Yes, you may be able to cope, especially if you have the same sort of experience as Tom from a previous career, but parishioners may find it very confusing, however well you as a priest seem to be managing the situation.

There can also be the insidious issue of apparent favourites, while others may feel ignored or rejected. If Samantha entertains only other young mums, childless people can feel left out. If Tom has a particular ministry among young people and spends most of his time with them, then older members of the congregation may get the impression that they do not matter.

Matthew Well, you seem to have demolished this curate pretty comprehensively.

Martyn I'm afraid the incumbent should also have considered the implications when he said, 'I want us to be best friends.' Actually their relative positions preclude friendship that is any more than what you would hope to have as colleagues in a boss–subordinate situation. At its worst, a constantly shifting and highly manipulative oscillation between 'I'm your friend' and 'I'm your boss' accompanied by inconsistent relationship signals could be a symptom of bullying. This can leave one with a feeling of disorientation. One curate said: 'I never knew which training incumbent was going to open the door when I arrived for the weekly planning meeting, so I never got it right.'

The curate needs to identify the patterns and use available support resources to help defuse the dynamic and then develop appropriate strategies. By the way, curates can be just as guilty of this, so when we talk about bullying, let's not just assume that it is always the training incumbent that we are talking about.

The fact is, though, that however cordial the relationship may be, the incumbent is in a position of authority over the curate. The priest must be sufficiently detached to be able to correct the curate, and when the time comes the incumbent must be able to write objective reports and references, which may not always be positive.

Beau May I come in here, Martyn? I think there's another point to be made. Think about what I was saying about professional adolescence. While we all hope it won't happen too often, it is essential that the curate should be able to be at odds with the training incumbent, sometimes quite strongly, and do whatever it takes to push the boundaries as far as they will go. I have come to see that if a curacy doesn't cross that threshold, from childlike compliance at the beginning, through turbulent adolescence, and eventually to a more confident, priestly maturity, then it can restrict the potential of that curate's life of ministry, sometimes to a highly debilitating extent. Worse, it becomes self-perpetuating if the curate subsequently becomes a training incumbent and models only the behaviours he or she observed and experienced when a curate. So I'm with Martyn on this: a curate should be friendly by all means, but should think very carefully before a friendly demeanour should be allowed to become a fuller friendship.

Matthew So the moral of the story is: be friendly, but don't be friends? It sounds rather bleak to me, but then I wasn't called to priestly ministry. So we seem to have arrived at another paradox: in order to create the right relationships, to be approachable and to serve, the curate has to learn to maintain healthy boundaries and keep an appropriate distance.

Beau and Martyn Correct.

Points for reflection

Curates

- How well do you understand boundaries?
- How does your view of ordination colour the relationships you make?
- Do you (and your family!) understand the tensions surrounding forming friendships?

Incumbents

- What have been your own experiences of having friends within the parish, both good and bad?
- What direction do you give, and what example do you set, about the tensions surrounding forming friendships?
- How do you integrate the family of the curate, not just the curate himself/herself, into the parish and help them to establish networks?

Dioceses

- What guidance do you give on friendships, other than policies for if things go wrong?
- What training and guidance do you give on boundaries in general?
- What is your approach to supporting clergy families, and how proactive are you about it?

5

I know it's your day off, but . . .

———•··•◆•··•———

I once heard a congregation member describe a vicar as a 'lazy toad' behind his back. The person had not even the slightest idea of quite how long and hard the vicar actually worked or what a typical working week looked like. The reality for the vicar was that there was no such thing as a standard working week. The only limit to his availability was the number of hours in a day and he had the greatest difficulty in saying 'no'. Many clergy and their families will identify with this exhausting way of life, and also, sadly, with the experience of being criticized without any basis in fact, or empathy. This type of pressure has a knock-on effect on family life and has the potential to cause breakdown and illness. It is little wonder that it is one of the things that curates find most difficult to manage in their new role. Here's a story that illustrates the problem.

There was a banging at the door of the curate's house. George and his wife Sally froze, hoping the person would give up and go away. They had been planning how they would spend this day together for ages. It was not easy for Sally to get a midweek day off from her job at the local health centre. They had really been looking forward to their trip up to London. After a visit to the Royal Academy they were going to have a relaxed lunch and then go to a matinee before taking the tea-time train home. That would give George time to change before the house group he was leading. They were already running late: the schedule for the last week had been blown out of the water by two funerals and having to cover for the vicar who had had a family bereavement. Now George was behind on a piece of written work that was due with the diocesan training officer, and they had had to delay their departure while he finished it and sent it off. The phone had rung several times, but they had let it go on to the answering machine after checking the caller display. Mrs Prendergast could wait for a couple of days.

The blinds were down at the front of the house; everyone knew it was his day off anyway – it was printed in the parish magazine and most people respected it. The banging continued relentlessly, however; whoever was there was clearly not going to go away. They looked at each other and shrugged their shoulders, and George rose to his feet and opened the door. Mrs Prendergast.

'I tried calling a few times but nobody answered, so as I saw lights on I knew you must be in. I know it's your day off, but you did promise that we could discuss the flowers for the patronal festival in September now that Christmas is over.'

'Ah yes. I agree we need to get down to that some time, but as it's only January, I wonder whether we might put a date in the diary to discuss this when we both have a little more time.'

'Oh, I don't have anything to do now, and as it's your day off I assumed you'd be free.'

And so it went on. George finally shut the door on Mrs Prendergast with a promise that he would call her later in the week, then he had to go and add this to his already impossible 'to do' list to make sure he didn't forget. When he came back to the living room, he could hear the warning signs. Sally was making crashing sounds in the kitchen as she piled up the breakfast things to wash up later. She was not happy.

'Why couldn't you have just told her to go away? You're always far too nice to people like her.'

'Well, I did try.'

'You didn't try hard enough. You let them bully you sometimes. You have no idea how hard it was for me to arrange this day off. And now going up to London just feels like too much trouble. You gave her priority over me. As usual!'

With that she stormed out of the room, slamming the door behind her.

By the time they had made their peace, which they always did, but not without tears and recriminations, they had missed their train and would be lucky to fit in a quick lunch before the theatre. As they hurried on the ten-minute walk to the station, George's mobile phone alerted him to a text message. Sally snorted as he stopped and read it.

'Oh dear. How sad! Mavis has had a stroke. I have to go and visit her at the nursing home.'

'No, you DON'T!' screamed Sally, making no attempt to keep her voice down. 'Why can't the vicar do it? Or the reader? Or someone else? Why does it *always* have to be you?'

At which point she started sobbing and turned for home. George followed disconsolately in her wake. He couldn't blame her. He just wondered why nobody had discussed issues like this when they were at theological college. He had always known it would be a busy life, but had imagined his previous career as an international marketing manager would have been good preparation. If only he had known the half of it! He wasn't alone: barely a meeting of the Ministry Development Group went by without one curate or another bemoaning how tired he was, or admitting how out of control she was feeling.

Matthew When I think back through my professional life, I can remember extended periods of working very long days for weeks at a time, living out of suitcases, or working at home late into the evening, neglecting my family, failing to use all my holiday allowance and so on. Some of the demands came from my employers, from the need to satisfy customers, the schedules of team projects and more besides. But I was my own worst enemy too. If I was highly energized by a project, I became totally immersed, my mind engaged almost to the point that I would dream about some aspect of it and wake up with the answer. I don't say this to glorify myself, but simply to make the point that working long hours isn't exclusive to clergy. Highly elastic working hours and conflicting 'must do' priorities are common to many professions. David Suchet put it succinctly when writing of filming *Poirot* for television:

> I had to leave home every morning at 6.30 a.m. and I often didn't get back to Pinner until 8.30 or 9 p.m. I'm afraid that meant that Sheila and the children didn't see a great deal of me in the months between July and Christmas 1988, because even when I did get home, I had to look at the script for the next day.[1]

So when I read about George and Sally, I have mixed feelings. I can certainly understand curates feeling oppressed by the onslaught of unfamiliar work in a new setting on top of continuing study obligations and in many cases the upheaval of a new home. At the same time, many newly ordained curates come from a life with similar, irresistible demands on their time. So what are the particular dimensions of ordained ministry that may make this pressure so difficult for curates and their families to accept?

Martyn It's largely one of perception and distorted realities. Parishioners have a way of assuming that the clergy are available on a round-the-clock basis and are unfailingly glad to be so. The assumption is often extended to include the family of the curate.

There's another dimension to it as well. The distortion comes from the fact that parishioners often think that what is important to them will be equally important to the clergy (and their family). In some ways, many parishioners can unintentionally conflate their personal relationship with God with that to their own clergy – who are often assumed, subliminally, to function as 'agents' of God. In prayer, people can bother God with minutiae and details about their lives all the time. I don't mean this observation as either critical or patronizing. But people in prayer may tell God lots of details about family, friends, aches, pains, anxieties, concerns, issues – any matter, indeed, that weighs on their heart or mind. And those who might pray like this can easily slide into assuming that their clergy will be just as interested in their lives, sometimes giving clergy detailed accounts of anything from a recent holiday and its problems through to the complexities of their daughter or son's new job.

Mrs Prendergast and the flowers for the patronal festival is one example. Another is the young man who telephoned the vicar at 7.15 on the morning of Boxing Day to say that he and his girlfriend had got engaged the previous evening. Wonderful news of course, but . . . 7.15 a.m. on Boxing Day? I'm sure that clergy could provide many such examples from their own experience, relating to just about every aspect of church life. This is something that the curate has to get used to, and yes, it is different. For most people in other working environments, communication is ring-fenced by working hours or by the use of company emails and office mobile phones. It is also bounded by business matters of (usually) mutual interest and content. Thus curates may think that they have seen it all before, but believe me, it is a whole new world and something that they and their families need to get used to.

Matthew So are you saying that curates should just put up with it? Or that things could be handled differently to restore some balance, health and sanity to their lives and that of their families?

Beau I'd like to suggest that Mrs Prendergast's behaviour, so typical of someone or other in just about every congregation, is a form of bullying, and it needs to be addressed if the curate is to develop any resilience. It requires a bit of nerve, but it simply has to be done – and, by the way, it has a strong theological basis. In the old ordination service, the priest is given authority to forgive, but also to retain sins. The Church doesn't often explain how to retain. How does this work?

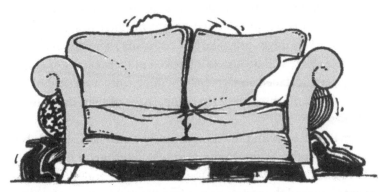

'Remember when we used to use the couch for having a cuddle?'

Rather than hiding behind the sofa when Mrs Prendergast stands at the door ringing the life out of the bell, the curate goes to the door. Opens it and says to the parishioner: 'This is my day off.'

The parishioner says, 'Oh, I know that, it's just a quick question ...'

Clergy person: 'It ... is ... my ... day ... off,' and keeps staring. 'Yes, but ...'

'It is my day off. I'll be happy to talk on another day.'

'Oh, I am so sorry. Please forgive the intrusion.' Departs. Hopefully, spreads the word.

Matthew That sounds brilliant, Beau, but it raises two questions. What happens if the training incumbent ('the boss') has a tendency, however dysfunctional, of always being available? Doesn't that create a conflict of perceptions within the parish, which is liable to be directed negatively at the curate? And might that in general colour people's perceptions of the curate as being lazy, however hard she or he works on the other six days of the week?

Beau There is that risk, but it's a risk the curate has to take. It is a manifestation of professional adolescence, but is only damaging if others, especially the incumbent, react with anger. If it's dealt with in a businesslike way, and above all with consistency, then it will be worth the short-term pain.

Martyn I agree, and I'd like to add a practical note to this. Life at theological college is not just about training, essay writing and the like, it is also about helping ordinands – and their families as far as is possible – to get a feel for what life will be like, the changes they may have to make, the relationships they will have to form. This is sometimes easier for students in residence than part-timers, but the principle applies to everyone. To take one example, compulsory chapel attendance is not just governed by the sort of 'ought' that you might expect in a theological college. It's about helping the students to get into a rhythm, learning to shape their day, so that whatever else may occur, worship lies in the context of that framework. The same is true of mealtimes, chapel serving rotas and other aspects of the community life. Of course, all that is a pale representation of the realities of life as a curate, but it is a start, and some students find even that a challenge. The ability to say 'no' to the things that fall outside these constraints is part of the process of learning about boundaries, and it is also part of developing a shield against the bullying tactics that some people employ to get their way.

Matthew When you talk about the schedules and demands at theological college, it does indeed sound like a calculated attempt to instil a sense of what life will be like as an ordained minister. That's ideal for residential students, but given that more and more training takes place on a part-time or distance learning basis, how can this aspect of formation be applied to all people entering ministry?

Martyn That is a major challenge because training institutions are constrained by their limited exposure to the ordinands, and even more so because they rarely meet the families. Thus, when we ran residential weekends and summer schools that are integral to that learning path, we used to apply the same principles, albeit in small bursts. There was a sense that it was community in microcosm, even for that short time. Timetables were structured, tasks were shared and a pattern of communal worship provided a rhythm. Many students are especially challenged by how to manage time, since they are often still in secular work with the wear and tear of commuting, as well as juggling family responsibilities.

Matthew In the story, I had sympathy with George, of course, but waving the flag for clergy spouses, I have even greater sympathy for Sally. It seemed as if the church came first and the family counted for nothing, even when they had gone to such great lengths to plan their day so that they could be together. I'm not surprised she cracked. If they couldn't get that sort of thing sorted out during their curacy, what hope is there for their married life together?

Beau Thanks for that opening, Matthew! I often surprise people when I say that the life of a married priest is a life of bigamy. Think about it: the priest has made two vows, both to God. One is at marriage, the other at ordination. They are equally sacred and require to be nurtured alongside each other. Sometimes it works very well, but at other times severe strains develop. It sounds as if this is only the start of a rocky road for George and Sally, and I suspect that this apparent conflict of loyalties is one of the main reasons that some clergy marriages get into difficulty.

Matthew Yes, the first time I heard you talk about the twin vows, and especially referring to it as bigamy, I was rather surprised, but then I remembered a conversation. A woman was sitting in the cathedral waiting for the ordination service to start. The organ struck up, and the procession wended its way down the aisle, with the ordinands in cassock and surplice.

Beau Yes, for all the world looking like a procession of brides.

Matthew Exactly. She said that her calm suddenly disintegrated and she almost screamed with rage: 'He's marrying God!' Even relating this a number of years after the event, her sense of outrage was still palpable. Is that what you had in mind?

Beau Yes. And the trouble is that the curacy may make matters even worse before they can get better. Consider this: the curate may be spending far more daytime hours with the training incumbent than with the family. It cannot help but be an intense relationship, even if it does not go through the professional adolescence I have already mentioned. Quite apart from a feeling of desertion, there may also be a definite hint of sexual tension and even threat. In this case, just suppose if George's training incumbent were a woman. I am not for one moment suggesting that curates, training incumbents and curates' spouses regularly get embroiled in a love triangle, but the relationship between the families can take on just that sort of dynamic, even if it doesn't end up in bed. And by the way, it can happen, arguably even more insidiously, the other way round: the incumbent's spouse may feel an equal sense of challenge and encroachment, especially if the two are ensconced in the incumbent's office in their home for hours at a time. The less quality time couples get to spend together, the more sacred such opportunities become. They can take a long time to plan, and not come along very often. I'm not surprised that Sally exploded when, yet again, George allowed their plans to be derailed.

Matthew Isn't it all part of the job? Shouldn't George and Sally have realized?

Martyn Actually, the flexibility of the life of ministry is the envy of many people whose working day starts on the 6.15 a.m. commuter train to London and only ends when they get home long after the children are tucked up in bed. The seemingly relentless workload doesn't have to be part of the job, at least on a constant basis. Some clergy learn very early in their ministry to block off time together and safeguard it. I know of clergy who do not answer the telephone or open the door between 4.30 and 7 p.m. so that the family, including the children, can guarantee something approaching normal family life.

Matthew Are you saying it's a matter of choice? That George could have ignored Mrs Prendergast, and left his mobile telephone at home?

Martyn Yes, precisely.

Matthew I think there's a lot that could be done with a few techniques that are easy to grasp. This isn't the place for a comprehensive survey, but here are two that I have found very helpful.

The first is the 'urgent and important' matrix, which would certainly have helped George to clear the decks for that day trip to London. How do you prioritize everything on your 'to do' list? After all, they can't *all* be the most important, the most difficult or the most time-consuming, and they don't all have to be done immediately. If you categorize everything on your 'to do' list, you might end up with a chart that looks a bit like Table 1, though obviously much busier.

Table 1 The urgent and important matrix

IMPORTANT but not Urgent	URGENT and IMPORTANT
Plan service rota a year ahead (*It is a 'must do' task but could be updated on a rolling basis*)	Meet the bishop in 30 minutes! (*It might be career-limiting to be late or miss the appointment*)
Neither Urgent *nor* Important	URGENT but not Important
Reformat the parish magazine (*Someone else can do it if it really needs doing!*)	Go to library before it closes (*Yes, it closes at 5 p.m. but it will be open again tomorrow*)

Of course, you may have different ideas of what constitutes urgent and important, but at least it gives you the opportunity to sift and prioritize, and to practise saying 'no'. While this will appeal to some and not to others, it's worth trying at least once: you'd be surprised how often you will discover that you regularly do the things from the bottom left, 'neither urgent nor important' square because they are quick and easy and give the illusion of progress and achievement. Actually, what you are really doing is piling up more and more pressure for the things that really matter.

That leads to another useful exercise, which I call 'What would happen if . . . ?'

I recall a time at work when there was nobody available to write a particular weekly report. So we asked ourselves what would happen if we simply didn't do it. We waited for someone to complain when the report wasn't issued. Nobody did and we dropped it permanently. I'm not suggesting that you should drop the 8 o'clock service each Sunday just because only three faithful people turn up, but it is amazing how many things in church routines seem to happen because they happen. Only inertia stops anyone from challenging them. As often as not it's left to the clergy (or their spouse!) to do whatever it is, but not doing it is often the better response.

But back to George and Sally. Are we perhaps being overcritical of their difficulty in finding their way through this time-management

*'Why did Mrs Jones ask me, at the church door, if
I ever formally trained as a hypnotherapist?'*

minefield? Is there anything else we can suggest to help them cope with all the pressures?

Beau People were always asking me if I was free to do this or that. I didn't like pretending, so every so often I would write the word 'something' in my diary. Then if somebody asked me if I were free I could truthfully say, 'Sorry, I have something in my diary that day.'

Matthew And that really works?

Beau Yes, though it probably won't do so any more after this book is published!

Matthew But the principle stands: if you ring-fence time in your diary then at least that time is sacrosanct, however busy you are at other times. My wife and I have found that the only way of making sure we are free at the same time is to go through the diary three months ahead, putting in a 'date day' at regular intervals.

Martyn It doesn't always have to be planned, though: a sense of spontaneity can help. My wife and I are often so busy that we seem to go for days at a time without having a proper conversation. I remember one day, to our astonishment, that neither of us had anything in the diary that evening, so we dropped everything and went to the cinema and had a wonderful time.

Matthew I wonder if the process of finding a way through time pressure is simply another dimension of the journey through professional adolescence.

Beau These time conflicts and the bigamous relationship certainly combine as major challenges to a curacy, so unless the curate establishes a strategy for confronting them face to face, the fallout when the explosion happens – and I say when, not if – can be destructive, to the curacy, the marriage and the church. I would say that finding solutions or strategies are key components of successfully attaining professional adolescence.

Matthew Doesn't this largely come down to the personality types of the people involved? Everyone is different, so their personalities will, of course, make a difference to how, if and when issues like these are resolved. Perhaps the greatest challenges might come if the curate and training incumbent have strongly opposing personalities and very different working preferences. For instance, bringing it back to George and Sally, what might have happened if they were both committed to respecting their day off as sacred, but the incumbent insisted that George must be available at all times and never say 'no'?

Martyn That again raises a range of issues about how training incumbents are chosen and trained, how a title post is decided on for a curate, and the care with which a curate and a training incumbent are put together.

Beau That's true, Martyn, but it also raises the importance of boundaries and is an aspect of bullying, which we have already started to explore and will discuss further in the next chapter.

Matthew And all that because Mrs Prendergast ruined George's day off!

Points for reflection

Curates

- How well established are your boundaries?
- What time management tools work for you, and what else could you try?
- Do you view holidays and days off as optional or non-negotiable?
- How do you set about preserving and protecting personal relationships, including the health of your marriage?

Training incumbents

- What behaviours do you model about protecting holidays, days off and protecting your marriage?

- If a curate used assertive behaviour with over-intrusive parishioners to establish boundaries, would you consider it good practice or as a black mark?
- What teaching do you give your congregation about the purpose of a curacy?

Dioceses

- What resources do you offer to help people develop time management skills?
- How realistic are your demands in terms of IME4–7 in relation to the other time pressures on a curate and their need to maintain sensible work–life balance?
- How, if at all, do you use personality profiling tools to match curates and training incumbents?

6

The workplace bully

When I was at boarding school, position in the pecking order was all-important. One of the first things I was required to do was to learn by heart the 'house order': the list of everyone in our house, being careful to give initials *before* the surname for prefects, and initials *after* the surname for sub-prefects, and just surnames for the rest of us. Critically, it had to be word perfect and in the right sequence. Within a peer group even having a surname with a higher position in the alphabet was sufficient to confer seniority. Should problems arise in day-to-day life, it was always the version of the more senior person that would be believed. I would like to say that it was different once I started my career in industry, but my experience was that the pecking order still mattered, though it was perhaps reflected slightly more subtly.

What has this got to do with curacies? Everything and nothing. You might imagine that in an organization based on Christian values, there would be impartiality, fairness, and facts discussed on their merits. Read on.

Audrey read the letter with relief. She was to be moved from the parish in the middle of her curacy. It had been a long haul, but now rescue was at hand. Only with hindsight did she realize quite how long ago it had all begun, even before the curacy actually started.

Towards the end of her final term at theological college Audrey finally identified her title post, as assistant curate in an Anglo-Catholic parish. It would mean moving, but she was single and had few ties. The only person she met when she went for an interview was the priest, Father Michael. He was faultlessly correct and polite, and he carefully explained about the parish, how he saw her curacy and the administrative details that needed to be shared, all very methodically. The organization of his office reflected that, with nothing out of place, everything in order, almost uncannily so. When he took Audrey to visit the church, she saw the same thing: none of the mess you normally see in the children's corner, the notices on the board very neat and tidy, but somehow not much of a 'feel' to the place. At the end of the interview she almost missed her train home because they had to go back to the church so that Father Michael could make sure he had locked it up properly. She also had to wait while he tidied everything on his already fastidiously neat desk before he was content to leave, locking the door with much ceremony.

Audrey valued detail and the correct ways of doing things, something she had learned at home as her father had been prone to anger. But once she started working, she found that Father Michael took this art to a whole new level. Somehow it seemed to affect his priorities. It became obvious that *how* you did something was more important than *why* you did it. This was obvious in the way he interacted with people, even in his sermons. They were theologically correct, of course, but they didn't inspire and didn't warm the heart. To be honest, they seemed to come out of a rather sad place. A pattern began to emerge: he was not just fastidious in a general way; cleaning and tidying seemed to be a compulsion. One day she accidentally put a book upside down in his bookshelf. He sprang out of his chair to put it the right way up.

It wasn't just her. One day he asked her to sit in on a meeting of the churchwardens and the sidesmen, which turned into a diatribe on the apparent lack of orderly arrangement of the hymn books and prayer books at the end of services. It would sound funny if it were not so sad, and indeed she noticed the churchwardens exchanging a smile; they had heard it all before.

There was another aspect to this: he could be downright aggressive, not to mention unpredictable. One day he would be open to having meetings with her, the next he would withdraw, almost pretending she wasn't there. Again, he might chat on the telephone about something, then ignore emails. On one occasion he denied that she had left a message on his answering machine when she was certain that she had, and she began to notice how many messages, emails and notes went unanswered. When it came to her training, he knew perfectly well that she was going to do a diocesan module on weddings, but he would not let her anywhere near the weddings taking place in the church, even as an observer, so she was denied the opportunity of arriving at the workshops with the same preparation that all the others had. As time went on she also noticed that he didn't ask her to preach as often as at the beginning, and comments and criticisms started coming back to her third hand, suggesting that he was talking about her behind her back, and not in a supportive way. He rarely gave her feedback, good or bad, and her self-confidence started to unravel.

She tried to bring things into the open, but he invariably responded by standing in front of her, shouting and gesticulating wildly, as she sat in silence, quivering and frightened. At other times, when she was simply trying to be helpful, he accused her of trying to manage him. However frightening this could be, she almost found this behaviour easier to bear than his times of silence, the lack of supervision sessions, exclusion from meetings and generally being treated as if she didn't exist. She could not even relax when Father Michael was being pleasant and reasonable, because that behaviour, too, was so unpredictable.

For a while she felt able to cope. After all, she had learned at an early age that the easiest way to avoid her father's wrath was to be meek, mild and compliant at all times. She was only going to be there for three years, whereas everyone else in the congregation was stuck with him. She could see how unhappy and lonely he was: he needed help. But she was also aware that it was changing her as a person, and not for the better. She discussed the situation with her spiritual director who was greatly disturbed on her behalf and recommended her in the strongest terms to take action, if only for her own protection.

This led to a meeting with the IME officer, who sympathized, but reminded Audrey that a curacy was an opportunity to learn how to cope with difficult situations. She advised careful thought before impugning the reputation of a training incumbent with so much experience, let alone invoking the bullying policy. Only with the greatest reluctance did she finally accept Audrey's conviction that Father Michael's behaviour had crossed a line of acceptability and agreed that she had a duty to take it further. Thus she found herself, 15 months into her curacy, in the bishop's study. And now, ten days later, the bishop, having made enquiries and considered the facts, had made his decision.

With immediate effect, she was to be attached to another parish on a temporary basis until a new context could be found for her curacy. She could start again! In the meantime, Father Michael was referred to the pastoral care advisor, because he, too, was clearly in need of help.

Matthew I'm amazed that Audrey lasted as long as she did. It sounds incredibly lonely and almost dangerous. If Father Michael had been around for so long, how come nobody knew that he was at the least a bit on the obsessive side, and also that he mistreated people so badly?

Martyn The truth is, of course, that they *will* have known. That the diocese chose to do nothing up to that point, but rather entrusted yet another curate to his care, is probably down to denial and collusion, with a bit of inertia thrown in. And what a failure that it took a crisis like this to get help for Father Michael as well.

Beau I agree. What confronted Audrey here was someone with a specific and nameable condition, obsessive–compulsive disorder, which manifested itself in a number of different ways, including bullying.

Matthew But before we get into that, how could someone like Father Michael possibly have been entrusted with oversight of a congregation, let alone the supervision of a curate in training? Even if only for his own benefit, he should not have been subjected to this extra stress.

Martyn I've already mentioned denial and collusion. Being in parish ministry can be a lonely job. Beyond the limits of the local team, there is sometimes little sense of diocese-wide collaboration or opportunities to mingle with others. Even events like deanery chapters and archdeacons' visitations are either too short or too infrequent for people to form a real view of the life and welfare of their colleagues. They are generally too busy and too preoccupied by the minutiae of their own day-to-day lives. Always assuming that Father Michael attends these peer-group events – and many clergy don't – it's unlikely that anyone would see the underlying signs of something wrong. This isn't the place to talk about diocesan oversight of the welfare of clergy in general, although there is a lot that could be said. What is clear, as I mentioned earlier, is that the allocation of a newly ordained curate to a title post is a critically important activity. Too often, as in this case, it is left to the curate to find a title post, with virtually no real knowledge of the prospective training incumbent and little guidance from the diocese. Each time a curate finds his or her own title post, it is a tick in the box, and one fewer problem for the diocese.

Matthew That's rather depressing. It suggests that a diocese intervenes only if something exceptional occurs, and even then with the greatest reluctance, and possibly after major damage has been done. It reminds me of efforts to get traffic lights or changes of speed limit in suburban streets: generally the council only acts if there has been a fatality.

Beau Yes, I'm afraid that is the case. Many of the people who come to see me clearly needed help long before I got to meet them, but I cannot help if I don't know there's a problem, and I am powerless to intervene on the basis of hearsay. Often nothing happens until a drama has turned into a crisis. Fortunately, Audrey realized the way things were going and took action to pre-empt an all-out emergency. In fact, despite the unsubtle and inappropriate warnings of the IME officer, having the courage to raise the issue with the higher authorities was not a failure, but the triumph of insight over habit in lessening its influence on her.

Matthew So let's think about Audrey, the curate. Was there anything she could have done when she went for the interview that might have opened her eyes to the reality of the situation she was getting herself into?

Beau A curate who walks into an interview expecting the training incumbent to be perfect in every sense will very soon be disabused. I concede that Father Michael's difficulties were extreme, and to be honest I am rather surprised that the incumbent was given that training responsibility. Audrey was in a very difficult position and I wouldn't wish such a situation on anyone. But, maybe putting such an extreme example to one side for the moment, you could argue that ministry is about handling challenging dynamics almost every day, whether within the leadership team, in the congregation or in the wider community. Without that experience in her tool-bag, she will simply not be equipped to do her job. With it, provided she survives the experience, she will be able to handle a wide range of pastoral challenges in a way that dear old Christopher in his so-called perfect curacy never would.

(Both) 'Since coming here my beliefs have definitely changed: I now believe in the doctrine of fallibility'

Matthew Yes, another of your dichotomies, but there are limits: we'd all agree that she should not have had to endure this sort of treatment. So, if she shouldn't have been allowed anywhere near Father Michael for her title post, who failed her? Her theological college? The diocese? The bishop?

Martyn Cases like this crop up more than they should, even with all the work that has been done by the national Church and dioceses to tighten up on selection and preparation of training incumbents. They are rarely as dysfunctional as Father Michael, but some of them still do not have the aptitude for taking on this responsibility. Maybe it happens because that parish has always had a curate, and there was no vetting of an incoming incumbent's suitability following an interregnum. Some of it comes down to the pressure under which ordinands find themselves – the pool of potential title posts seems to evaporate as ordination gets closer. People can't then choose the ideal position, but instead select the 'least worst' option, very often the only one that is available. In a case like this, it can leave the curate isolated and without any local source of help.

Matthew I often wonder about churchwardens. On paper they have pretty strong powers. Isn't it their duty to intervene when something like this is going on?

Martyn In theory you're quite right, but the reality is that churchwardens are often unaware that they have these powers. Even then, they would mostly be extremely reluctant to intervene in a conflict between two clergy. Most of all, though, there is tacit denial. Even if they know, they would really rather *not* know, and hope it will sort itself out in time. In the same way, even if the bishop and archdeacon are aware that something is amiss, they would prefer not to know officially, because then they would have to act. It's *mokita* again: what everybody knows but nobody says.

Matthew Fair enough. Audrey was there whether or not she should have been. Let's turn back to her account of events. Father Michael was clearly displaying classic signs of bullying. Helena Wilkinson usefully defines bullying as follows:[1]

> Bullying is not the occasional burst of anger, unkind word or thoughtless action: it is persistent intimidation, criticism, control, manipulation and misuse of power. However cleverly it is disguised, and sometimes it is well hidden behind a façade of care, bullying is abuse.

Beau Yes, it was bullying, and this is a good and clear definition. Of course, gender, age and level of experience may all play a part in the bully's selection of a target. Bullying may be more ingrained in some cultures than in others, which can make it more appropriate to focus on treatment than on avoidance. Bullies don't choose indiscriminately; they find out who is susceptible and target them. Audrey was just such a target, whereas it sounds as if the churchwardens were not, however frequently Father Michael gave them a hard time.

Matthew It seems to me that we are in a cleft stick. Nobody knew that Audrey was susceptible to bullying, so no one was prepared for it; and nobody knew it was going on so they didn't know help was needed. Weren't there aspects of the training process that should have triggered action?

Martyn In theory, yes. This is one place where the bureaucracy of IME4–7 might have come to Audrey's aid, because the health of the curacy process is judged on recorded evidence to demonstrate progression towards attaining competencies. Wholesale gaps in the evidence will be a strong clue that something is amiss and that the fundamental relationship with the training incumbent may not be going well. Reviews should give visibility of this. The trouble is that usually the diocese only sees these reviews once a year, and may not have the time to reflect in detail on what is *not* down on paper. This is all the more true because external moderation of year-end reviews is part of the process, and external moderators obviously don't know the people involved. And in any case, even if the problems were picked up in this way, a huge amount of damage may have been done by that point.

Matthew Something for dioceses to think about, perhaps. As for Audrey, how come she lasted so long in this environment?

Beau The trouble is that Audrey never actually cracked up. That sounds callous, but what other than a crisis was going to invite outside scrutiny? If she had broken down then it would have forced the issue and intervention would have followed rapidly. Instead, she was almost too nice, responding with exceptional charity to Father Michael's behaviour. My concern is that if this initial experience doesn't result in a change in the way she responds to bullying, be it through counselling, reading books on the subject or some other intervention, then the pattern is liable to recur, because she may be fundamentally susceptible to bullying. Why? Because in her new parish there may very well be someone waiting to pick on her. It may not be the training incumbent, but perhaps someone like Mrs Prendergast from Chapter 5, or Connie, whom we will meet in Chapter 8, or someone else.

'Aaaargh!'

Matthew Is there anything that could have been done during her training that might have helped Audrey?

Beau The key thing is to encourage the curate to set personal boundaries in an appropriate way, and to respond to the degree that those boundaries are challenged – not excessively, but appropriately. In most situations, this will provide protection against incursions. And learning about those boundaries should be in the basic kit of everyone entering a life of ministry. The trouble comes if that basic armour is not enough, for instance if the boundary incursions become persistent and aggressive. Then the response may also have to be more on the aggressive side.

Matthew You mean fighting fire with fire?

Beau Not exactly. At one time I was seeing a lot of people (a good many of them curates) who had been bullied. It was the relentlessness of the bullying behaviour, combined with the assumption that as they were clergy they necessarily had to take a placatory stance, just like Audrey, that left them feeling trapped and wondering if they could go on with their ministry, feeling as put down as they were. Part of the problem was not knowing there was an alternative – of always having to be nice.

So common was this problem that I ran a workshop for clergy on how to handle people who test you by being confrontational. It incorporated some transactional analysis skills and material from the many books on the subject.

After presenting a variety of approaches in dealing with difficult behaviour, I invited the clergy to role-play the part of their own worst nightmare people, and a colleague would try out these different approaches, with an observer to lead the reflection and discussion afterwards. The clergyperson was encouraged to continue in role until the particular approach that had the greatest effect on countering the negative behaviour was identified. Then there was an opportunity to put into practice the most effective antidotes, until they came naturally.

Matthew In other words, developing and practising a repertoire of appropriate responses that work in different situations?

Beau That's right. Let me give you an example from earlier in my career. When I first came to work in a psychiatric hospital, a bishop came on a visit. The chaplain and I took him to the staff canteen for lunch, during which the bishop became very loud and aggressive towards me. His arrogant put-downs were attracting the attention of fellow staff eating at nearby tables. The conversation went backwards and forwards, with him piling insult upon insult, while I listened, taking careful note of what he said. I chose my moment and quoted back to him verbatim what he had said. I told him that I had far better things to do with my time than play his game of one-upmanship, and walked away from the situation.

Matthew But isn't that simply a game of 'I'm better at bullying than you are'?

Beau I can see how it may come across in that way, but I saw it not so much as a put-down on my part as a rite of passage, learning to take a stronger role in my own ministry. It also established my reputation at the hospital. The bishop in question subsequently treated me with the care and respect of one carefully tiptoeing through a live minefield. The public embarrassment and knowing that it would be reported elsewhere meant that he couldn't continue with his arrogant behaviour.

Matthew So the message to Audrey and people like her is to hit back? Perhaps easier for a six-foot something with a loud, assertive voice and the moral high ground of subject-matter expertise, than for a newly ordained curate in a very vulnerable subordinate position confronted by someone like Father Michael in a line management role. And all the more so when she is effectively trapped in her curacy for three years.

Beau I know you are sceptical, but it really is possible to help someone to respond to bullying behaviour in a few short sessions, and I promise you that it really works.

Matthew What about this business of being ignored, kept out of meetings, never receiving any feedback, being treated as if she didn't exist?

Beau Yes, that's another aspect of bullying, and it's insidious because the realization of what is happening creeps up on you unawares, and sometimes it's been going on quite a long time before you realize the diminishing effect it is having on you. And it's all the more damaging if episodes of this sort of behaviour are intermingled with times of cordial interaction that suggest that nothing is wrong and that the relationship is in perfect order.

Martyn Described this way, it comes across as a comprehensive dismantling of the victim's well-being.

Beau Yes.

Matthew You suggested that, assuming she knew what was going on and had been trained, Audrey might have stood up to Father Michael's shouting and gesticulating by the appropriate use of words, responses and gestures. I can see how that might work when she had something to push against. But how should she respond in the vacuum of being ignored, when there's nothing to push against?

Beau Yes, that's more difficult, but the same principle applies. It's a question of choosing the opportunity. It doesn't just happen, though; it has to be learned and practised, whether on courses or in one-to-one sessions.

Matthew I can see how these techniques might be employed if the victim realizes at the time what is happening and the effect it is having on him or her, but I can equally imagine situations where it is only with hindsight, perhaps with outside help when things have gone badly wrong, that the victim starts to understand what has been going on.

Martyn The point you are making, Matthew, is the vital one. If people don't know what they are confronting, then they cannot be equipped for dealing with it. At theological college we certainly taught about boundaries, but there was less about bullying. Before we start rewriting the syllabus, though, in reality the Church is not full of habitual bullies. Yes, there are those who could do with some people management training and need to do work on boundaries, but that is not a reason to have an all-out assault on what might be a rather more isolated problem.

Matthew But as we have seen, it is not just clergy who can make life miserable for other clergy. Congregations and the wider parish contain their fair share of bullies too.

Martyn Yes, that is true, but at least interactions with those people are only part of the mix, outnumbered by the far greater number of well-functioning working relationships that most clergy experience.

Beau I agree, Martyn, so we need to understand ways in which the lack of robust boundaries and the emergence of bullying behaviours sometimes progress from being an upsetting nuisance to becoming an all-out emergency precipitating the need for intervention, support or even separation. This is about cause and effect. If bullying and other forms of abusive behaviour are the cause, then the effect can be something called 'projective identification', or PI. In the simplest terms it is what happens when the mud sticks and changes the person on the receiving end.

Let's look at projective identification[2] first from a positive point of view. If sufficient people say encouraging things sufficiently frequently to a person who suffers from self-doubt, that person will eventually begin to identify with what is being said, and it will change the individual's self-perception. This can be successfully facilitated in group sessions with professional help.

Matthew That makes sense, and now you mention it, I can think of occasions when I've seen it happen. Success all round. What about negative PI? Audrey realized that Father Michael's bullying behaviours were not only getting to her, but were beginning to change who she was, and she shouted for help.

Beau Yes, that's why I brought it up here. But let's be clear: I'm not talking about the odd occasion when people get their timing or wording wrong or blow their top. I'm talking about absolutes – a continued and intensifying pattern of negativity and hostility. When that happens, it's highly likely that the person's ability to function will be compromised and rapid intervention is called for. On occasions where I have encountered this in a therapeutic setting, I have generally been on the telephone to the bishop within the hour to advise him that this person needed to be moved instantly, out of harm's way.

Martyn But keeping things balanced, Beau, this surely doesn't happen very often.

Beau No, that's why I talk of absolutes as opposed to degrees on a continuum, but it might surprise you to know that this can even happen in the world of the therapist. Faced with a client who continually throws out comments like 'you're no help', there is a strong risk that some of the negativity may stick and dent the therapist's ability to operate. You might think a therapist should be able to cope with it, but I promise you that in such a situation we are trained to terminate the therapy instantly, for our own safety.

Matthew So, Audrey experienced bullying in varying forms and there are techniques she could have adopted to counter it, if only she had known and had the training. It reached a tipping point when she began to believe the negativity and lost her ability to operate. We call this projective identification. How fortunate that she called out for help before it was too late.

Points for reflection

Curates

- How do you react to bullying behaviours among those around you?
- What resources, policies and courses are available to help you?
- At what point would you seek outside help if you felt you were being bullied?
- How are you engaging your support network as a safety valve?

Training incumbents

- Are you aware of how your behaviours come across?
- Would you know if you were crossing the line between assertiveness and bullying?
- Are you ever subjected to bullying behaviours, and do you know where to find help?

Dioceses

- How much do you research the history and nature of newly ordained curates and of potential training incumbents before you pair them for a curacy?
- If rumours of bullying reach you unofficially, what is your default reaction and action?
- What courses and resources do you have to help people understand boundaries and to recognize and combat bullying?
- How do you deploy pastoral care advisors, how well known is the service, and what advice are they trained to give in cases of alleged bullying?

7

Working agreement?
What working agreement?

In most walks of life there are documents that govern ways of working. It may be a simple job description, or something more elaborate that specifies the tasks to be undertaken, limits of responsibility, formal working relationships and so on. The detail varies. Some are codified for a specific process that must be followed to the letter, for instance in regulated or scientific environments. Others may be of minimal value, especially for people in wide-ranging senior positions, or for those who work largely by themselves. I recall my executive contract, which stated: 'Office hours are 37.5 hours per week, but you will be expected to work whatever hours are necessary to achieve your agreed objectives.' Game, set and match to my employer!

In curacies, the governance document is usually called a working agreement. It may vary in different places, but a typical list of topics covered would be as follows:[1]

- mutual expectations
- supervisory and working arrangements
- allocation of time
- worship
- spirituality and personal development
- structured learning and reflection: professional development
- team working
- pastoral responsibilities
- time off and annual leave
- progression and monitoring
- other support and conflict resolution.

Agreements may be formally signed and witnessed, and examples of best practice abound. They are most powerful when they are organic, changing as the curacy evolves, and are used as key inputs to monthly supervision, annual review meetings and the end of curacy assessment. All very responsible and methodical.

Sadly, though, however much is put in writing, an agreement guarantees nothing, for two reasons. First, it may not say the right things. Curates may feel that they have to agree to things that they may be unable to deliver. For example, a self-supporting curate dividing the working week between the church and secular employment may feel obliged to take on more commitments than he or she will have time for. This ought to be the subject of fruitful discussion at reviews, but that does not always work out, as we see in the case study that follows. The other reason, also covered in the case study, is that sometimes things are written down because they have to be included, but with no intention of taking any notice of them; instead they are consigned to the depths of the filing cabinet to be forgotten. Let's hear about Gareth.

Gareth had thought of going into the Church for some years, and was already serving as a reader in the church that he and his wife had attended for years, where the children had grown up and now returned with their own children. This provided him with flexibility about how much or little he did, though he had always felt that he wanted to do more. The only thing that really held him back from responding to the call to priestly ministry was his health. For some years he had been treated for a mild heart condition: nothing life-threatening provided he managed his time, kept stress under control and took plenty of time to rest and recover after especially arduous periods, whether at the office where he worked part-time or in the church. After reflection and prayer, discussion with his family, and consultation with people such as the vicar, the vocations advisor and his spiritual director, he decided that the time was right to take it to the next stage.

From the start of the discussions with the Diocesan Director of Ordinands (DDO) his health came up, and they had a long and searching discussion about whether his active ministry might be better restricted to the more flexible and less gruelling regime as a reader. Gareth took time to consider that, but the call would not go away, and the DDO agreed to progress his application but explained that even if the bishop approved, he would still need to be examined by the diocesan medical officer. He had no difficulty with that, and the medical officer's report supported Gareth, but with provisos about working hours, the number of engagements he took on, recovery time and, above all, the requirement that he should work part-time on a self-supporting basis.

The medical situation wasn't raised when he went to the Bishops' Advisory Panel (BAP) except as a reference in the final written recommendation that he should be permitted to undertake training but that any active ministry should take full account of his health. Thus he completed his training, undertaken on a part-time basis, and started his curacy in a different parish, though one within reach of his home. All started promisingly, and Gareth got on well with Alex, the priest in charge. Although Alex had not been a training incumbent before, he seemed to have a good instinct for how it should work and a cordial and fruitful working relationship looked highly likely.

Early on in the curacy, they completed and signed a working agreement. Gareth was possibly his own worst enemy at this point. He agreed up front to do more than he could really manage, but pushed himself anyway, carried on a wave of enthusiasm – his own and Alex's. In fact enthusiasm, energy and drive lay at the heart of Alex's ministry. He was ever available, worked incredibly long hours, was indefatigable and had all the benefits of possessing a strong and vibrant personality.

It couldn't last.

One day, Alex phoned Gareth and asked him to take a funeral at very little notice, on top of a week that was already
a long way beyond his agreed hours. Of course Gareth said
'yes', but then half an hour later realized that this was simply
impossible and called back and said that he couldn't do it after
all. The suppressed angry silence at the other end of the phone
was almost tangible. Not long after that, there were meetings
with the IME officer and the bishop, all undertaken with the
best interests of the church in mind. In the meantime Gareth
was given leave of absence for rest and reflection. It was an
extended process and the eventual outcome was that the
curacy was terminated. Gareth was given permission to officiate
within the diocese, but his record was marked to show that he
had not completed his curacy.

Matthew At the outset they had agreed and recorded a route that
would honour Gareth's ministry, while reflecting the constraints
imposed by his health, and testing these limits within the relative
safety of a curacy. All bases were covered, so it must have been
confusing for Alex to receive mixed messages: Gareth needed
kid-glove treatment because of his medical history, while at the
same time he kept saying 'yes' to everything.

Martyn I think it depends on how it was done. In a way this is
bringing us back to the discussion of the emerging Church of the
future and an apparent conflict of assumptions and approaches.
For many people the old paradigm is alive and well . . . curates
are inexperienced, fully deployable, young, probably unattached,
in full-time stipendiary ministry and so on. This tends to be accompanied by a one-size-fits-all approach in terms of both ongoing
training and formation, and attitudes, expectations and assumptions.
Gareth, like increasing numbers of others, has a completely different profile.

Matthew Yes, he's highly experienced, he's not deployable, he's mature, he's married with children and grandchildren, he's in self-supporting ministry and he's part-time. Added to that, he's in poor health. If you are right about the old paradigms lingering, how come he was recommended for training?

Beau Because things happen at multiple levels. The Church has been ordaining a rich mix of people for years. The introduction of female ordination added greatly to that richness. Regardless of your views on that, the broad mix is exactly what the Church needs. With the old paradigms, though, we are talking about subliminal assumptions that continue to colour decisions, planning and much else. It's an uneasy tension: the Church is a bit like a car with a pull to one side. However much you want to steer a straight line, you're always compensating for that pull. Sometimes we let the pull take us in the wrong direction, sometimes we resist.

Matthew In other words, we are not talking here about the nature of policies and guidelines themselves so much as the way people interpret them in the light of their own thinking and experience.

'I felt like asking the churchwarden whether he happened to notice that my dog collar does not come with a lead attached'

Martyn Exactly. There's nothing wrong with that list of working agreement contents, and as it stands there's nothing prescriptive in it. What makes it a useful document are four things.

- Is it accurate and does it reflect what has been agreed between the training incumbent and the curate?
- Is it workable and practical? Stretch targets are fine and generally healthy for everyone, but unattainable ones are counter-productive.
- Is it regularly monitored? Many such documents end up signed then consigned to a drawer, gathering dust until the next annual review.
- Is it kept up to date, modified in the light of experience, perhaps with modifications to work commitments or new targets?

Matthew That sounds a bit like the SMART acronym, which prompts us to ensure that the individual components of a working agreement are specific, measurable, achievable, realistic and timely.

Martyn Yes, so in Gareth's case the problem was that although the working hours were specific and measurable, and it was timely in the sense that it referred specifically to the period up to the next annual review, they were neither achievable, in view of his health, nor realistic in terms of the context of his part-time ministry.

Matthew But Alex wasn't an ogre. How come these expectations found their way onto paper? And how come he went on pushing for more, even beyond the already unachievable and unrealistic goals on the document?

Beau There are several things here. Let's start with the most human and obvious one, for which nobody could really be blamed. As a parish priest, the training incumbent is already impossibly busy, stretched by demands from all quarters. On top of that, the curacy sucks in a huge amount of time and energy. It's not surprising that anyone in that situation would want to share the load, so however much we may buy into the idea that a curate is not simply a spare pair of hands, what could be more natural and understandable than to use the curate exactly as that?

Matthew Is there any sense of exacting revenge on the curate for making the training incumbent so extra-busy?

Beau That's possible for some, yes, but at a very deep level, and it is not something of which any of the parties would generally be aware.

Matthew So we are not returning to the discussion of bullying here?

Beau No, not really, although in other hands the situation could have turned nasty, if the training incumbent became frustrated and effectively blamed the curate for being exactly what he had always said he was, rather than fitting to the subconscious paradigm. I have come across cases fairly like this where the curate, perhaps because of years of being defensive about her health, was a natural target for a bully. In that case the demands were almost deliberately cranked up. In the context of transactional analysis, Eric Berne would have called it playing the 'I told you so' game.[2] Pressure is intensified until the failure that was always expected does eventually happen, at which point the training incumbent, fully vindicated, can say, 'I told you so!'

In that same case, the training incumbent had told the bishop early in the curacy that the person wouldn't ever end her curacy, and was eventually proved right, but only by piling on more and more pressure until the prophecy was fulfilled. That was a bullying relationship in the sense that the training incumbent was subconsciously playing the same game back, with none of the 'crossing' that is needed to make relationships change onto a more wholesome footing. In my language that is where professional adolescence comes in.

Matthew But that's not what we are talking about here, is it?

Beau No, it's not, but I thought it important to slip that in, if only to differentiate between the working relationship between

Alex and Gareth on the one hand and genuine bullying relation-ships on the other. So let's move on to the other dimensions of this.

As I have already mentioned, one of the essential parts of a curacy is learning how to do things, and generally the only way of learning is by doing, making mistakes, doing them again, until they become second nature. So when you told me that one of your research panel complained that he had had to conduct over 100 funerals, I was not unduly perturbed. In this case, though, the extra funeral seemed like an opportunity to the training incumbent and a threat to the curate.

Martyn We have to remind ourselves about the importance of boundaries too, when it comes to time management and workload. It's not just a question of what is or isn't in the working agree-ment. On top of the SMART objectives, there needs to be con-sistency. It's no good saying 'yes' today and 'no' tomorrow. That doesn't help either the training incumbent or the curate; nor will it help the curate to manage time effectively in the next stages of ministry.

*'I am a bit puzzled why the incumbent suggested
I prepare for my first Parish Council meeting
by watching* Prime Minister's Question Time'

Not for nothing does Jesus say: 'Let your "Yes" be "Yes," and your "No," "No".'[3] Anything else is just plain unhelpful in the long run. It also makes it increasingly difficult for the training incumbent to know what to expect of the curate.

Matthew Surely that works both ways? There are plenty of scatty and disorganized training incumbents out there making life almost a lottery for some curates.

Beau Yes, that's true, but at the risk of sounding callous, that's all part of the rich pattern of ministry. Curates might as well find out now rather than later that the only thing they will be able to control in their life of ministry, working with volunteers, part-timers, unpredictable parishioners and bureaucratic dioceses, is themselves!

Matthew So are we saying that a working agreement isn't worth the paper it's written on?

Martyn By no means. It exists as a working document, there to serve and prompt and provide a framework, but on no account to be a straitjacket. If it doesn't help and provide healthy stretch and manageable objectives, it probably isn't saying the right things. And if its existence is purely another tick in the box to satisfy IME4–7 without adding any further value, it might as well be ignored altogether.

Matthew So in this case, it's all about the working agreement saying the right things and the use and respect of boundaries, and nothing directly to do with the curate's ill health.

Martyn Yes, because the Church isn't stupid. It wouldn't allow someone to be ordained if it didn't believe that the person had a ministry that could be exercised in a sustainable way. Thinking pragmatically as well, the investment of selection, training and formation, not to mention ongoing curacy costs, is simply too immense for a positive BAP recommendation to be made on the basis of sympathy or sentiment.

Beau So as usual, we have a paradox. A working agreement is a useful and important tool to help provide a framework; but its strength comes from knowing when to use it, when to update it, and when to ignore it!

Points for reflection

Curates

- Do you see the working agreement as a help or as a chore?
- How do you respond to being asked to do things that exceed the agreed terms of your working agreement?
- What techniques do you have to help you assert your needs while maintaining the flow of the curacy and parish life?

Incumbents

- Do you see the working agreement as a help or as a chore?
- In what circumstances would you ask the curate to do things that are in excess of the agreed terms of the working agreement?
- How frequently do you refer to the working agreement, and when would you consider updating it?

Dioceses

- Do you see the working agreement as a help or as a chore?
- What guidelines do you have for the effective use of working agreements?
- In what circumstances do you look at individual working agreements and assess their effectiveness as curacy documents?

8

Day 200: still at sea

---◆---

And so to our last story. Everything seems set fair. The training incumbent and the curate are comfortable with each other, and have found a professional way of expressing and resolving any differences as they move forward. They are managing the training requirements without undue difficulties and they are coping with the stresses that are normal in any curacy. In short, the first seven conversations will have had little to offer them that they don't already know. And then everything changes. Abigail, the curate, takes up the story.

If you had asked me how I would define the perfect curacy, it would not even have come close to how ideal it all was at St Peter's under Bob's brilliant leadership. He seemed to have the perfect way of helping me to balance the work and the training and the settling in. Even when I got things wrong, he generally smiled and used it as a learning opportunity. And he was always heavy on praise and encouragement too. That's what made the monthly supervision sessions such a success. And although we had different perspectives on ordination and churchmanship, we managed to accommodate each other quite easily. Did we have any rows? Yes, of course we did, and that was not always easy. I do have a bit of a temper, after all, and I'm not too happy to think back on the way I behaved once or twice. But he didn't react there and then. Sometimes I wished he would, but he let me work it out. As I say, not always easy at the time, but I somehow came out of it more rounded, with some rough edges knocked off and hardened up.

That's just as well.

One day, halfway through my second year, Bob called me in and told me that he had been to the doctor. I knew he had been having tests, and now he said he had the results, and the news was not good. It's too painful to go into all the details of his illness, but he deteriorated rapidly, and soon I was carrying a lot of the burden of running the parish. As long as he was at home, he wanted to be involved, but I knew that the best thing for him was to focus on his own health and well-being, so I tried not to bother him any more than I needed to.

Everyone rallied round, and the area dean did his best to lighten my load with visiting clergy from time to time, but that was not always possible. The real trouble was that for many I was the person they came to for consolation at the sadness, and later the bereavement, that they all felt. There was nobody there for me. And my supervision sessions had stopped months before, of course, so at the very time I needed extra support, I actually had nobody there with whom to discuss and share and offload on a day-to-day basis.

Spiritually I felt the gap just as badly. Bob and I had developed a rhythm of saying Morning Prayer together almost from the beginning of the curacy. They were good times, with our focus totally on our relationship with God, recharging our batteries, you might say. And even if we were going to have a meeting afterwards, he would always make sure we had a cup of tea between the two, so the boundaries were very clear. Yes, it could not have gone better, which is what made it worse when Bob became ill and eventually died.

At first the diocese made a big effort to help. You could not fault the bishop and the archdeacon. Both visited Bob regularly, and the bishop conducted the funeral. From a pastoral point of view they did everything you might have expected, and more. The problem was that with all the extra work I had to do in the parish, I had little time for my own grief, and I started to fall behind with my training. Spiritual direction? Oh yes: Mavis was and is wonderful, but I only see her every six weeks, and in any case she's not there to manage my training. Actually, she has always made a point of standing at one remove from all the detail, which has meant that these times with her are like a spiritual oasis. There was only one churchwarden, and he was very inexperienced and therefore couldn't help much. My circle of friends outside the parish, sadly some way away, were invaluable, grounding me in the reality of the world. They were shoulders to weep on, whether face to face or on the phone, and ordinary things like outings and shared meals helped to maintain a balanced view of life.

The IME officer was aware of what had happened and offered a little latitude around the expectations for submission of essays and portfolios, and he arranged for a vicar in another parish to act as supervisor. Unfortunately, though, Father Christopher, a lovely man, had a totally different churchmanship from mine, and he had never been a training incumbent. In any case he had an incredibly busy schedule and so found it hard to fit me in, and I was just as busy myself. The reality was that from the beginning of Bob's illness to the end of my curacy, a period of a little over 18 months, I had only one supervision session. As I was working flat out just to keep on top of everything that had to be done, my training really came to a juddering halt halfway through my curacy.

Matthew What a sad story. Let's pause first to celebrate the working relationship that Abigail had with Bob. What an amazing training incumbent he seems to have been!

Martyn Yes, indeed. I would consider any curate fortunate who had a training incumbent like Bob. And although people like to throw stones, I believe that the majority do come pretty close to that, one way or the other. This situation was especially sad, but I hear all sorts of variations on it.

Matthew Yes, I know what you mean. The stories I came across in my research included other cases like this, but also less traumatic interruptions like job changes, promotions and other life transitions. The common factor in each is a hiatus in the curacy, sometimes very sudden, at other times more drawn out.

Martyn Yes, it's not unusual, so we have to make the best of it.

Matthew But isn't the intention that the curate and the training incumbent should form an enduring partnership for the full length of the curacy?

Martyn It's the ideal, yes, but the practicalities of life don't always fit our ideals. The reality of this is even reflected in the Ministry Division guidelines referred to earlier, which state: 'The training incumbent will make a commitment to stay for the curate's diaconate, and expects to be there for the majority of the four year training period.'[1] In other words, the commitment to be there during the diaconate lasts only for the first year. However firm the expectation and however strong the resolve, the fact is that *force majeure* can strike suddenly and in unexpected ways: sometimes, as with illness and bereavement, against the will of all involved.

Matthew So if it happens so often, shouldn't the Church, whether nationally or at a diocesan level, have this covered?

Martyn Yes, it should, and in many cases a smooth and satisfactory transition takes place.

Matthew My nervousness about this lies in the way the Church continues to move from pastoral models towards managerial or human resources based approaches. Policies and procedures are available on most diocesan websites, but after a career in industry,

I recognize the human resources wording framed to cover every eventuality, but expressed in a way that seems protective of the organization rather than of the needs and welfare of the curate. Thus I read in the same document you have just mentioned that the guidelines 'should complement and signpost the Diocesan Handbook or wherever clergy terms and conditions for the Diocese are to be found'.

It sounds good, because it gives the impression of providing the support mechanism that is needed, but even the expression 'clergy terms and conditions' sounds mechanistic and impersonal, and therefore incapable of getting to the heart of the unique nature of ordained ministry.

Beau I agree with that, Matthew, and I share that nervousness. And the trouble is that the Church does not have the experience, whether specifically of human resources, or of all-round organizational management. This means that the Church is beginning to talk the language without necessarily understanding its implications or knowing what to do with it.

Matthew So, in the case of Abigail's curacy, put into limbo for reasons beyond her control, we might expect a mitigation plan to be in place, but the Church might not know how to implement it in the smooth and practical way that the world of industry would achieve, however impersonally they might do it.

Martyn I hate to say it, but I have seen plenty of examples of industry handling people issues better than the Church. Basically I agree. The mitigation plan should be in place.

Beau That's all fine, but I think we need to get down to some rather more fundamental issues. In Abigail's case, you might say that what happened was the making of her, however sad it was. Fine, she didn't have to go through professional adolescence in quite the ways I have already described, but she went through a severe time of testing and came out safe and sound the other side.

*'Why do I suddenly feel so devastated? I'm getting what
I've always wanted. The incumbent is leaving and
I will be the only priest left in charge'*

Matthew Do we know that, Beau? What about her studies and her general development as a minister and everything else that is meant to happen during a curacy?

Beau You're right: there may indeed be some holes in the programme of training and formation that had been mapped out for her. Some of that can be remedied later, but at an emotional and relational level, I still believe she is likely to thrive better in her ongoing ministry than many who had a continuous working relationship with their training incumbent from beginning to end.

Matthew Yes, I can think of at least one curate who managed to glide through an interregnum with total security and serenity. But not everyone is like that, and I have come across others who felt bereft, cast adrift; and, frankly, they entered the next stage of their ministry unprepared, in practical, emotional or spiritual ways, especially if they were then moving to a position of responsibility.

Beau That's true, but I would like to add another strand of thinking here. In terms of systems theory, the curacy relationship is a 'system' in which the training incumbent is the 'parent' and the curate is the 'child'. If there is a disturbance or distortion of that 'system', then, all being well, something will enter to fill the void and restore the system to functionality. Thus, an extremely experienced curate may be able to weather the storm; or the diocese may intervene rapidly and appoint a stand-in training incumbent who has the capacity and experience to continue the training work at an appropriate level and quality. In both these circumstances, it may indeed be true to say that a time of testing during an interregnum or other interruption will actually have helped the curate.

Matthew Are you saying that dioceses shouldn't have ways of helping more proactively?

Beau Not at all. I am simply saying that however much help is or is not given, this period of change may not necessarily be a disaster.

Matthew Yes, I can see that, and however traumatic and upsetting the experience may have been for Abigail, she did seem to come through it. But interruptions to curacies seem to happen so often, and in so many ways. Let's test how systems theory works with two other examples.

> Graham, the training incumbent, had an emotional breakdown and went to see the bishop, who agreed a period of absence. In order to make the arrangements for how this would work in practice, the bishop had a meeting with the two churchwardens. Although Paul, the curate, was aware of the meeting, he was not invited, and was told by the churchwardens that this was because it was they, not Paul, who were in charge during this leave of absence. The bishop did not communicate with the curate, nor was there any discussion of how supervision should continue during the training incumbent's absence. Paul, who had an especially close working relationship with Graham, felt devastated by his exclusion.

Martyn The first thing to say about this is that under canon law, the bishop and the churchwardens did the right thing. Indeed, it would have been wrong to burden Paul with overall parish responsibility during this difficult period. One might comment on how it was handled pastorally, but that is a different question.

Beau In terms of systems theory, that is actually the nub of the problem, Martyn. Don't forget that when an incumbent is installed in a parish, the bishop says, 'Receive this cure of souls which is both mine and thine,' meaning basically that the buck stops with the bishop for everything that happens within the parish – and that includes the healthy running of the curacy, if there is one. In this case, the bishop did nothing to restore the 'system' and the curacy suffered.

Matthew Whether we talk at the level of systems theory or of diocesan processes, Graham was the one who lost out. It shouldn't have happened, and could have been avoided. The word 'devastated' is pretty strong, so I hope that Graham's support network was robust and able to carry him through the experience.

Let's look at the other example.

Ruth, the vicar, was successful in gaining an appointment in a different parish. Andrew, the curate, saw this as an opportunity to see how he would get on during the interregnum. However, Ruth was hardly out of the door before Connie, the part-time NSM[2] and a retired headmistress, muscled in without any authority from anybody and more or less took charge, organizing everything, pouring herself into the work, all the while wearing a martyred expression on her face. Instead of having the opportunity to fly and taking on more responsibility, Andrew actually found himself with less to do as Connie marginalized him and the rest of the leadership team.

Beau This is actually an example of what is called theme inter-ference. Let me explain. When something unexpected happens in a team setting, it can raise a lot of strong feelings that take every-one by surprise. This is usually less to do with the external situation itself than with what it unearths beneath the surface: often an unresolved team conflict that is relatively harmless as long as the team structure remains intact, but which may turn into 'sibling rivalry', especially if the head of the hierarchy leaves. That is what happened here. All along, Connie might have been nursing a deep desire to be a 'proper vicar' herself, so she seized this opportu-nity to take charge, destabilizing the whole team, not just Andrew's curacy. As in family dynamics, it awaits an authority figure to re-correct and redefine the hierarchical boundaries blurred by the 'coup' and put everyone back in their designated space so that the rivalry does not triumph by poisoning the parish atmosphere. This realignment by the authority of proper boundaries then makes the team feel secure.

Matthew That all makes sense, and, as you say, it is the sort of thing that can occur in any team, not just in the Church. But it's worth stressing that an interregnum is often seen as an enjoyable

Who gets the yellow T-shirt for 'Fastest Rescuer in the Parish'?

challenge rather than as something negative, providing the opportunity for new talents and gifts to come to the surface in a very constructive way. As we have seen, though, that is not always the case, so I wonder how dioceses could help to turn these situations into the 'least worst' outcome for the health of the curacy.

Martyn It may be asking for something that cannot be achieved within the constraints of an already overstretched Church. The ideal would be to parachute in a stand-in training incumbent who is:

- experienced as a training incumbent;
- aware of current requirements and approaches;
- available for regular supervision, minimum monthly;
- flexible in churchmanship, understanding of ordination and general ecclesiology;
- committed to providing the required support.

Matthew Sounds good, but is it practical?

Martyn Of course not. It's like suggesting that there should be a full taxi rank round the clock just on the off-chance that there might be a fare in the small hours of the morning. The Church does not have the resources to provide support on this scale, so in the end we tend to muddle through situations like this, perhaps with some informal oversight from clergy in neighbouring parishes, but not on the scale required of a training incumbent. Sadly, this can leave scars – emotional, spiritual and practical – that last for a long time.

Beau May we return to Matthew's observation about the Church's shift from a pastoral perspective to a mechanistic, procedure-led organization? This can work if we have the right organization. But, as Martyn says, there are simply not enough people in the centre of each diocese to juggle the needs of overlapping cohorts of curates at various stages of their curacies. Maybe there is one IME officer handling the entire job, which is fine when everything runs smoothly. But incidents and exceptions, whatever form they take, are the things that suck in their attention, and they simply don't have the bandwidth for it.

Matthew So it's hardly surprising if the response of the diocese is to appoint someone – anyone, almost – to be a stand-in training incumbent, cross their fingers and move on to the next problem. It's almost as if they expect the curate to be able to cope and seem surprised if they do not.

Beau That's right. Though, as we have now seen, the test of whether the diocese has really done a good job of filling the void is if we can say that the 'system' has been restored. One way of characterizing what you have just described as crossing their fingers and moving on to the next problem is whether or not they have actually solved this problem; often, it appears, they haven't, because the system remains disturbed and distorted.

But there's another issue here. By its very nature, IME4–7 is mechanistic and prescriptive, and, as we have seen, has a heavy bias towards academic study and approaches. It is hardly surprising that the sort of person who is appointed IME officer is likely to be an academic, or someone who is qualified in adult education, or perhaps a brilliant administrator. That is exactly what the job requires in order to deliver what has been handed down, but may often come with minimal hands-on parish experience, which is something of a contradiction. The difficulty is this. Where the job is combined with a parish role, as happens in some dioceses, then answers to problems are likely to be grounded in the realities of the day-to-day life of ordained ministry. Where, on the other hand, the individual has no such contact, and indeed has minimal previous experience of parish ministry, then there is a risk that he or she might not be in tune with the dynamics of what is going on, and therefore not be equipped to help, even if time were available to do so.

Matthew Is that a swipe at IME officers and dioceses, Beau?

Beau No, but it is a reflection of a reality that at times feels strongly at odds with the needs of the Church and of the individuals who, let us remember, have offered the precious gift of themselves, often at a great cost to themselves and their families, when they enter ordained ministry. In the ideal world, an IME officer should have had personal experience of being a training incumbent at least once, as a prerequisite to doing that job from the centre.

Martyn I agree with that very strongly. The trouble is, in Abigail's case, that all the right pastoral help was there at the time of Bob's illness and death, but then other problems absorbed the attention of the bishop and the archdeacon. Don't forget the massive cost to the Church of selection, training and formation of a priest: interruptions to a curacy should not be left to chance. But in this case the diocese, while in theory fulfilling its obligations by appointing a stand-in supervisor, didn't check to see that it was working.

Matthew Abigail mentioned the importance of having a spiritual director.

Martyn Yes. Critical. I know that some people are uncomfortable with the name, because they see it as dictatorial. Fine: I don't care what you call it. Companion? Soul mate? Buddy? Actually I prefer companion: one we break bread with. Whatever you call it, being without someone to walk the spiritual journey alongside you should not be an option for a priest.

Matthew Actually, it seems to me that there are overlapping resources that might be useful. What about pastoral advisors, Beau?

Beau Yes. Nearly every diocese has a pastoral advisor, usually someone, like me, with experience or a qualification in counselling, therapy or a related discipline. They are available to clergy and their spouses for completely confidential consultation, often at little or no charge for the first few sessions. This is nothing to do with spiritual direction. In Abigail's case, for instance, it might have helped her to look at the bereavement she was unable to express within her congregation, and indeed might have shown her that it could have been beneficial to all if she *had* been open in expressing it. That's just one example.

Martyn And then there are work consultants, who help to look at processes and ways of working, and can help to establish new relationships. In Abigail's case, a session with a diocesan work consultant, perhaps with the churchwardens, might have brought useful results in working out what to prioritize, what could be dropped, how the laity might be engaged to fill the gaps, and so on. Again, quite different from the work of either spiritual directors or pastoral advisors.

Matthew Abigail mentioned her circle of friends. We have already discussed the challenges of having real friendships within the parish, so maintaining old friendships becomes all the more important for the curate, and equally so for the curate's family.

Martyn Yes, and some curates benefit from prayer triangles or cell groups that go back to their training days, sometimes lasting for decades.

Matthew We have not so far mentioned the benefits of having a mentor. This is an experienced person, usually from within the organization, who can give practical advice and suggestions on career progression, relationships and other areas that may be unfamiliar or difficult for the trainee. In industry, education and many other fields it is often the norm for a trainee to be allocated a mentor, but it's not something I have observed much in the Church. Are we missing a trick here?

Martyn No, I don't think so. Many of the ways that a mentor can help already occur naturally within a well-functioning curacy relationship. As the training incumbent is effectively the line manager, however, some issues may need to be explored elsewhere. This is where the spiritual director, work consultant or pastoral advisor comes in, though it is true that some people do find it helpful to have a dedicated mentor as well.

Matthew What we are underlining here is the importance of an established support network even when things are running smoothly, but especially so during an interregnum and other times of change or stress. And the fact is that despite best intentions, even the best curacy can grind to a halt for totally unpredictable reasons, and often does.

Beau Yes. Ideally the curacy should not be interrupted. If it is, then everything should be in place to provide seamless support for the curate. But we all agree that often doesn't happen: let's hope the curate comes through the experience unscathed. I know you think that I'm always looking for times of testing for the sake of it, but I really don't believe that an interregnum is an unmitigated disaster, despite the short-term discomfort, if the curate finds a way to cope and as a result develops greater resilience, flexibility and self-reliance.

Matthew Isn't that the point, though? Surely we should not leave it to chance whether or not the curate can cope in these circumstances?

Martyn No, and that is why we have been stressing the importance of the support network, and the challenge to dioceses to ensure that there is a contingency plan in place to provide seamless continuity.

Points for reflection

Curates
- How do you react to the idea that you may be left to 'fly solo' partway through your curacy?
- What support networks do you have in place?

- Are your time management practices sufficiently robust to manage the extra workload, especially if you have to take on additional tasks, while protecting quality time with God and your family?

Training incumbents

- When you take on a curacy, how committed are you to remaining in post for the duration of the curacy, in so far as that is in your control?
- When you know that there is going to be an interruption in oversight, what steps do you take to protect the flow of the curacy?
- Would the competence, nature or the personality of the curate make a difference to how you would handle an impending interruption to the curacy?

Dioceses

- Do you view an interregnum or other interruption to a curacy as a learning opportunity for the curate, or as a situation that requires diocesan intervention and oversight?
- When you appoint interim supervisors, how do you ensure that the arrangement is working?

A more excellent way

The inspiration and impetus for this book came not from dry facts, reports and statistics, but from the stories people told, some full of joy, fulfilment and success, others sharing times of pain, loneliness and disillusionment. Although we have taken the lid off some of the relational and psychological dynamics that underlie the experiences of curates and training incumbents, we now look forward with hope and optimism, starting and ending this chapter with words of encouragement. First, from Jacqueline Stober:[1]

> Hopefully your curacy will be straightforward and affirming. Public ministry does not always take place in a fridge, but in the warmth of God's loving care and the fellowship and approval of his people. But if you do sense the temperature beginning to fall, you really only need three things to help you through the difficult times: some very good friends who will love you and affirm your gifts; a foundation of robust spiritual practices such as prayer, meditation, reflection; plus a little faith that the God who called you will sustain you no matter what life may bring.

Matthew Lovely words, and a huge encouragement for addressing the ups and downs of most curacies. We should not, however, overlook the perspective of curates and training incumbents at times when they may be experiencing especially tough challenges, when hope and optimism may feel a long way off. Even such comforting words as these may not resonate, and practical suggestions offered with the best of intentions may jar. This is not because the words are not valid, or because the suggestions are not helpful. It is because the greater need at that time may simply be to feel heard and believed, and for the pain to be recognized.

Martyn Yes, we certainly owe it to everyone who has been through a troubled curacy to acknowledge their experience. Simply saying that the pain will pass or to suggest that such cases are extreme and in a minority does not ease the wrenching emotions and doubts experienced at the time; and in any case, as I suggested at the outset, it happens far more frequently than we would care to admit.

Beau I, too, can support that view, from a professional perspective. It is standard practice in therapy that one listens first, empathizing as the emotions emerge. Only when that need has subsided does one start gently to ascertain the facts, and eventually work towards solutions. All too often, out of a genuine wish to be helpful, people offer advice that has not been asked for.

Martyn Perhaps, because many people find it hard to cope with other people's raw and messy emotions, it can feel easier to fast-track to offering solutions.

Matthew So here's the rub. How shall we respond to readers who have been through absolute misery, who see no light at the end of tunnel, and feel that they have been irrevocably damaged by their experience? Isn't there a risk that by repeatedly suggesting that those times of testing are invariably the making of them, we may be seen to be offering glib answers showing that we have not heard the pain?

Martyn But we *have* heard the pain. We have shared stories typical of those that are so often untold. We have unlocked some important truths, which will help those experiencing difficulties now to recognize that they are not alone, that there *is* light at the end of the tunnel and that there *are* sources of help. We have shown that by adopting new techniques or adjusting some of their routines, sometimes in quite simple ways, curates and training incumbents can restore the equilibrium and move on. More important, for those at an earlier stage of the journey, I hope that we may have pre-empted many of these difficulties.

Matthew I may nevertheless have expected us to have provided more comprehensive and unequivocal explanations for a lot of common issues. Instead it seems that we have laid a strong trail of dichotomies and contradictions.

Beau Yes, I'm glad you noticed that. Perhaps some readers who have had bad experiences may have hoped that we would give them a public voice that will bring about change. I believe that the very existence of this book does just that. But rather than focus purely on the extreme situations that occasionally arise, and the associated pain and strong emotions, we have opted for a more encouraging message: that in most cases, 'hanging in there' is likely to pay dividends in the long run, however much of a short-term struggle that might represent.

Matthew Hence the priest who described her curacy thus:

> At the start: 'Honeymoon period? What honeymoon period?'
> In the middle: 'This is absolute hell. It's going to kill me.'
> A year later: 'It was the making of me.'

Beau Yes, exactly. So whether it is boundaries, the difficulty of an interregnum, calibrating friendships, managing time, developing strategies for dealing with bullying, or any of the other topics we have explored, it is frequently the case that working through the difficulties will pave the way to a more robust, secure and integrated future ministry.

Martyn That often means taking a risk, but it is one worth taking. I suppose St Paul draws the threads of this together when he says, 'My strength is made perfect in weakness'[2] – that it is through identifying, understanding and addressing our areas of vulnerability that we grow and flourish.

Beau But I sense that we haven't quite convinced you, Matthew.

Matthew You noticed? Well, earlier in the book we suggested that everyone is 'on the spectrum of something or other', but that it depends quite how far a person deviates from what one might call 'normal' before it affects the way they behave or whether or not other people even notice.

Martyn The word 'normal' is a subjective description and it can actually be unhelpful to try to define most curacy relationships in those terms.

Beau Yes, and the particular mix of our widely varying personalities, including our hang-ups and eccentricities, can be useful rather than, or as well as, being destructive. Here's an example: to train a spy you actually have to teach that person to be paranoid (if he or she isn't so already) in order to stay alive; but having been trained to be continually suspicious, the spy will never be able to turn it off. This is well illustrated in the John Le Carré novels, where none of the spies has a successful personal relationship at home.

Matthew So you are actually making a virtue of what may seem to be abnormal?

Beau Yes.

Matthew It does nevertheless occur to me that we have touched on personality disorders in the context of dysfunctional relationships, but we haven't gone into a lot of detail.

Beau No, and I'm not going to start now.

Matthew Is that because there's a risk that people will overreact to just about any eccentricity or foible, when all they really need is to learn how to relate to people who are different from themselves?

Martyn That's a good challenge, Matthew, because in my experience extreme personality disorders in the context of ordained ministry are relatively rare. The risk, though, is that in the rather isolated world of a curacy, there are few opportunities for outside recognition of these issues, and even fewer for intervention, so difficulties that might be defused with comparative ease in other contexts might, in a curacy, need a crisis to bring the problem into the open.

Matthew Perhaps that's why I *was* expecting us to offer a sort of idiot's guide to pathologies and psychiatric conditions. What I think you are actually saying is that we should instead focus on the tipping point, where the extremes of a person's personality become a nuisance and affect both the individual and others, especially in trying circumstances.

Beau Yes, that's right. The point to stress is that the tipping point that you describe almost always arises from a combination of the context and circumstances superimposed on the characteristics of the individuals concerned. It is really not very common for it to be occasioned by disorders and illnesses, and it would be a distraction to go too far down that road.

Matthew But I thought we were going to explain the psychology of curacies.

Beau And that's exactly what we have been doing, but not in the way you were expecting. Think back to Audrey's situation in Chapter 6, where we could have put the focus on Father Michael's obsessive–compulsive disorder. Instead our focus was on understanding and protecting boundaries, on watching for signs of bullying, and being aware of projective identification. All these may equally happen without a pathology being present. The key thing is to establish self-defence strategies to cope with situations if they take a turn for the worse.

Martyn In other words, balancing cause and effect. One of the great benefits of a curacy is precisely that of how the curate gets to grips with the intricacies of interacting with other people, starting with the training incumbent. And because every curacy is different, it's a continuous learning process, for the training incumbent as well. Most people learn to coexist by trial and error: that is a normal part of a curacy.

Beau Yes, I agree, but sometimes difficulties in establishing successful coexistence between two people can take time to emerge, regardless of the nature or extremes of their personalities, or any disorders they may have. In the confined space of a curacy, it can be hard to spot in advance someone whose personality lacks natural defences or has been damaged as a result of childhood trauma. They may look normal, but are actually putting on an act, effectively operating as an 'as if' person.

Martyn I guess your point here, Beau, is that sometimes, though really rather rarely, there are extremes that can only be explained by pathologies or personality disorders, that may require the intervention of a professional like you, and may require the training incumbent and the curate to be separated.

Beau Yes, and that brings me to my main point. Whether or not people are 'normal' is a red herring and is actually rather unhelpful for the vast majority of situations. The last thing we want to do is to set off 'medical students' syndrome', where the students begin to feel they have every disease they read about. To describe pathological conditions in the context of curacies invites a similar reflection: 'Does your curate/incumbent have this condition? If so, it could be dangerous: run, don't walk, to your nearest shrink!'

Matthew Is this where we meet the 'more excellent way'?

Beau Yes. In his work on pastoral care, Robert Lambourne makes a distinction between a *disease* (what is specifically wrong) and an *illness* (where the disease does a coup and takes over and becomes what essentially defines you as a person). Thus, one person may be in a wheelchair but without that defining who he is: his life continues in spite of, not because of it. This is quite distinct from someone who, say, had an industrial accident and whose pain and disability are so intrusive as effectively to define who he is. Perhaps a 'doctor, doctor' joke illustrates the difference:

Patient: 'Doctor, doctor, my family thought I should come to see you because I like pancakes.'
Doctor: 'Nothing wrong with that; I like pancakes myself!'
Patient: 'Great! Do drop round some time; I have 40 trunks full!'

Matthew And in the context of a curacy?

Beau So your incumbent likes to be organized? But to ask you, the curate, to write out all your sermons a year in advance? Or so your curate is a bit shy and introverted? But to stay in the house for 12 hours a day with the curtains drawn? The 'illness' perspective encourages a preoccupation with what's wrong, almost as an end in itself, whereas the 'disease' perspective encourages us to focus on the person, warts and all. This is a more pastoral approach.

Essentially we learn to live with and even use the different personality traits of others. It is a matter of degree whether it is an endearing foible, a pastoral problem, or a psychological condition needing attention, or even separation of the people concerned. So a personality clash may be anything from a useful and positive learning opportunity to a crisis causing misery for all involved. Nor are our differences fixed in time: since we all have kinks in our personality, what might be seen as creative tension at one point may feel like a train crash at another. It is usually impossible to predict: sometimes things like this can remain dormant and only brought to the surface by outside events like problems at the children's school, divorce, a car accident or a bereavement.

Matthew So, to summarize, curacies may get into trouble, but we should focus on accepting and valuing people where they are, and leave it to experts such as therapists to make a differential diagnosis if that is what required.

Beau Yup. This emphasis puts the focus on who we are and what we *can* do, giving the best possible opportunity for us to exercise our God-given gifts. This pastoral model sees everyone as God has made us, in our physical or emotional or spiritual weakness: the context of the adventure of life. When we think in these terms, then we can ride any storm.

Matthew Does that mean we have been wrong to take the lid off the difficulties and dysfunctionalities that are encountered in curacies?

Beau By no means. We still need to understand what is going on, and it is right to offer pointers and solutions wherever possible. But how much more effective it is when we focus our approach on healing, restoration and reconciliation, and indeed on everyday relationships, and on the individuals rather than their characteristics. That ultimately lets God in, when we so often use science and analysis to keep God out.

This was one of those days when the thought of filling up the font with gin and then drinking it did not seem altogether unreasonable

Martyn That feels a very positive way of facing the reality of curacies, whether as curates or training incumbents, as they live their life of ministry. And then, to use the words of Monica Furlong,[3] they can be grounded in a steady and affirming aspiration:

> I am clear what I want . . . I want them to be people who can by their own happiness and contentment challenge my ideas about status, about success, about money, and so to teach me how to live more independently of such drugs. I want them to be people who can dare, as I do not dare, and as few of my contemporaries dare, to refuse to work flat out, to refuse to compete with me in strenuous-ness. I want them to be people . . . who can face the emptiness and possible depression which often attack people when they do not keep the surface of their mind occupied. I want them to be people who have faced this kind of loneliness and discovered how fruitful it is, as I want them to be people who have faced the problems of prayer. I want them to be people who can sit still without feeling guilty, and from whom I can learn some kind of tranquillity, in a society which has almost lost the art.

Matthew Which brings me on to another . . .

Beau and Martyn Sorry. Your time is up.

Need help now?

Some things can't be worked through with people in your immediate support network. If you need urgent help straight away, here are three options to consider.

Confidential help within your diocese

Get in touch with Anglican Pastoral Care. The primary task of this organization is to provide pastoral care and counselling to clergy, their immediate families and others in ministry in the Church of England. The counselling offered is usually subsidized or paid for by the diocese, but it is completely confidential. The service may vary from diocese to diocese, and is usually available to you, and your spouse, whether separately or together.

Be careful about what you divulge about your situation when setting up your counselling: your first point of contact may not be a counsellor, but someone appointed by the diocese to take messages and pass them on to the counsellor.

Contact details at: <www.pastoralcare.org.uk/>.

Help away from home

You may need time out *now*, even *today* at a pinch. Yes, the parish *will* survive without you. Really.

The Society of Mary and Martha is an independent charity in Devon offering specialist confidential support to clergy and/or spouses. Programme events like 12,000-mile Service weeks are scheduled through the year. Linhay Lodges provide an emergency bolt-hole with one-to-one support especially at times of stress, crisis, burnout or breakdown. They aim to keep some short-notice availability.

Contact details at: <www.sheldon.uk.com>. Tel.: 01647 252752.

Loss of faith

This can be very scary indeed, the more so because faith is the bedrock of your vocation. Whether doubts are any more than the normal transient questions that we all ask, or a sense that the flame has been extinguished altogether, it is a burden not to be carried alone. This is where your spiritual director – who has possibly also suffered in the same way – may be of help. See 'Further reading' (see page 132) for a helpful book.

Top tips and resources

Your support network

Fortunately, most difficulties and queries can be resolved within your support network, which will consist of different people for different purposes. Figure 1 illustrates the various roles that offer the different sorts of support you may find you need.

It is possible that a single individual may fulfil more than one of these needs, but be aware of boundaries; where appropriate,

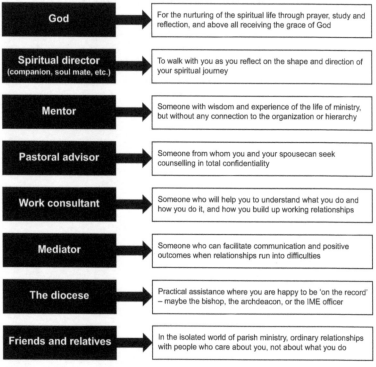

God	For the nurturing of the spiritual life through prayer, study and reflection, and above all receiving the grace of God
Spiritual director (companion, soul mate, etc.)	To walk with you as you reflect on the shape and direction of your spiritual journey
Mentor	Someone with wisdom and experience of the life of ministry, but without any connection to the organization or hierarchy
Pastoral advisor	Someone from whom you and your spousecan seek counselling in total confidentiality
Work consultant	Someone who will help you to understand what you do and how you do it, and how you build up working relationships
Mediator	Someone who can facilitate communication and positive outcomes when relationships run into difficulties
The diocese	Practical assistance where you are happy to be 'on the record' – maybe the bishop, the archdeacon, or the IME officer
Friends and relatives	In the isolated world of parish ministry, ordinary relationships with people who care about you, not about what you do

Figure 1 Your support network

agree the ground rules before you get started, especially where confidentiality is concerned.

There may be times when you will need to make a joint decision about getting someone else involved, for instance a work consultant to help you establish a working pattern, or a mediator should things become difficult between you.

Curates

When seeking a title post, weigh up the relative merits of key factors:

- churchmanship
- geography
- family needs (spouse's job, schools, dependent relatives)
- nature of training incumbent
- vision of host parish *vs* personal vision.

Remember that however senior you may have been in previous secular employment, your experience will only get you so far. This is a different environment, and you are here to learn.

Learn to say 'no'! But find a way of doing so that is engaging rather than leaving a bad impression. For example, 'No, I'm sorry, I'm afraid I won't be able to do that, but would it help if I did such and such, to take the load off you a bit?'

Manage time – learn to distinguish between urgent, important and neither, and prioritize accordingly.

If you are married, remember that your marriage vows have equal status to your ordination vows.

Ensure that you have a robust support mechanism in place.

Nurture your friendships.

Never be too busy for prayer and reflection. If you find yourself squeezing them out, then you need to look again at how you prioritize.

When you move in, remember that your family, if any, are also going through a time of change in a strange environment. Get the balance right between launching straight into the curacy and playing your part in making the house a home.

Agree ground rules as to:

- which part of the house is your exclusive work area;
- how the telephone, answering machine and email will be used;
- ring-fencing family time;
- how to deal with unexpected visitors.

Remember: your days off and holidays are sacrosanct!

Incumbents

Most training incumbents enjoy the experience, finding it fulfilling and a real blessing. The suggestions that follow are intended to help make sure that that is indeed the outcome.

Weigh up the implications

Before taking on a curacy, weigh up the investment of time and energy that will be involved, against both your existing parish commitments and your home and family life.

Since the curate is not a 'spare pair of hands', you are never likely to achieve the equivalent of two full-time clergy's work in the parish. One experienced training incumbent estimated:

Year 1: The equivalent of 1 person's work between the two of you
Year 2: 1.25 people's work
Year 3: 1.5 people's work

The curacy will involve you in training activities that may not seem personally relevant or a good use of your own time. These may include diocesan events for training incumbents; assessments, reviews and other paperwork; regular supervision sessions with your curate; and attending services simply to shadow the curate.

Decide how you will react to:

- the mistakes that the curate will certainly make;
- differences in matters of churchmanship and personality;
- rebellion, argument and conflict;
- the curate's relationships within the parish.

Manage time, tasks and support

Consider engaging a diocesan work consultant to work with you and the curate to help you develop the working agreement.

Consider what tasks you could put down or pass on to others to make sufficient space for the curacy.

Protect your days off, holidays and time for retreats. These are more important than ever and should be seen as non-negotiable.

Ensure that you have your own support network in place.

Dioceses

Before the curacy starts

- Be proactive in helping the right curate to be paired with the right training incumbent.
- Take particular care if the appointment seems a 'no brainer' simply because it involves least inconvenience.
- Proactively deploy a work consultant to support the curate and the training incumbent in the early days, especially when preparing the working agreement.
- Be aware that the arrival of a new curate will have an impact on the roles and perceptions of others in the ministry team: associate priests, readers, youth workers and others. They, too, may need careful preparation.

During the curacy

- Monitor progress, balancing IME4–7 requirements and pastoral issues.
- Be aware of family issues as well.

- Have a contingency plan in place for all curacies, to cover circumstances where the incumbent is no longer able to discharge the training duties, for example due to illness, career change, or personal circumstances.
- Monitor levels of supervision during any interval without a training incumbent to ensure that the curate receives proper and ongoing oversight.

If things go wrong

- Monitor progress as things proceed: there shouldn't be any surprises about this!
- Be prepared to parachute in a mediator if required.
- Have in place a plan for how to deal with broken curacies.
- Ensure that all parties are aware of the pastoral advisor in your diocese.
- Ensure that your bullying policy is something that lives, and is not simply a document on the website.

Congregations

Remember: a curacy is first and foremost a training position. This means:

- The curate is not a spare pair of hands!
- The incumbent is likely to be more busy, certainly at first.
- The curate will be required to spend time on non-parish activities including training.
- The curate is there to make mistakes and learn from them.

Give the curate and family time to get used to the major life changes they are probably experiencing, including changes of job and home, possible reduction in income, all on top of the sequence of vocation discernment, selection, training and ordination.

The curate, whether married or not, needs to get established in the new environment. Visits and offers of help may be welcome from the outset, or you may need to give him or her time and space; try to gauge which is right in your situation.

Do not make comparisons. The things that interested previous curates or that they were good at are completely irrelevant. Similarly, the curate may have particular gifts that are outside your experience: treat this as an opportunity, not a threat!

There is no role for a curate's spouse other than the promises made in the marriage service. Whatever your experience of previous curates' spouses, make no assumptions, but simply welcome the family as members of the congregation.

Don't assume that the curate's family will come to church. That must be their choice. And if it is a benefice, they may choose to go to one or other of the churches and not favour 'yours'. That too is their choice.

There's a difference between being friendly and being friends. The curate may find it takes time to calibrate the appropriate degree of friendliness. Assume nothing, and don't feel offended if your curate seems distant or spends more time with other people.

Further reading

There are many books and other resources that touch on different aspect of curacies. This list provides a taster.

Experiences of curates and training incumbents and their families

Jonathon Ross-McNairn and Sonya Barron (eds), *Being a Curate: Stories of What It's Really Like*, London: SPCK, 2014.

Matthew Caminer, *A Clergy Husband's Survival Guide*, London: SPCK, 2012.

Practical advice and guidelines

John Witcombe (ed), *The Curate's Guide*, London: Church House Publishing, 2005, revised 2009.

Rick Simpson, *Supervising a Curate: A Short Guide to a Complex Task*, Cambridge: Grove Pastoral Series, 2011.

Keith Lamdin and David Tilley, *Supporting New Ministers in the Local Church*, London: SPCK, 2007.

Helena Wilkinson, *Insight into Child and Adult Bullying*, Farnham: CWR, 2013.

Barbara Berckhan: *Judo with Words: An Intelligent Way to Counter Verbal Attacks*, London: Free Association Books, 2001.

Pastoral care

Gordon Oliver, *Ministry Without Madness*, London: SPCK, 2012.

Kate Lichfield, *Tend My Flock: Sustaining Good Practice in Pastoral Care*, Norwich: Canterbury Press, 2006.

Nigel Peyton and Caroline Gatrell, *Managing Clergy Lives*, London: Bloomsbury, 2013.

Loss of faith

John Pritchard, *God Lost and Found*, London: SPCK, 2011.

Broader perspectives

Yvonne Warren, *The Cracked Pot: The State of Today's Anglican Parish Clergy*, Stowmarket: Kevin Mayhew, 2002.

Tim Ling (ed.), *Moving On in Ministry: Discernment for Times of Transition and Change*, London: Church House Publishing, 2013.

David Heywood, *Reimagining Ministry*, London: SCM Press, 2011.

Church of England Ministry Division reports

Good Practice in the Appointment and Training of Training Incumbents, 2014.

The Trajectory of Vocation from Bishops' Advisory Panel to First Incumbency, 2011.

Formation and Assessment in Curacy, 2011.

Notes

Introduction

1 The two sets of opening quotations are taken verbatim from contributions to the research that led to this book. It is explained later in this Introduction.

2 Matthew Caminer, *A Clergy Husband's Survival Guide*, London: SPCK, 2012.

3 Jonathon Ross-McNairn and Sonia Barron (eds), *Being a Curate: Stories of What It's Really Like*, London: SPCK, 2014.

4 Tim Ling (ed.), *Moving On in Ministry: Discernment for Times of Transition and Change*, London: Church House Publishing, 2013.

5 IME4–7, Initial Ministerial Education Years 4 to 7, is the Church of England's name for the formal process of training and formation undertaken by curates following ordination. The previous name for this was Post-Ordination Training (POT).

6 *Good Practice in the Appointment and Training of Training Incumbents*, Church of England Ministry Division, 2014.

7 Papua New Guinean Trobriand Islands Kiriwina. It refers to an obvious truth that is either being ignored or going unaddressed, and also applies to an obvious problem or risk no one wants to discuss. It can be seen also as a 'polite fiction', a social scenario in which all participants are aware of a truth, but pretend to believe in some alternative version of events to avoid conflict or embarrassment. It has a similar meaning to 'the elephant in the room'.

8 Title post is the name used for the first parish appointment for a newly ordained curate.

1 The nightmare curate

1 The Ministry Division website advises of 48 BAPs per year, each normally with two groups of eight, making a total of 768 per year, stated here as 'between 700 and 800' to reflect any variation that may occur from BAP to BAP, and from year to year.

2 *Criteria for Selection for the Ordained Ministry in the Church of England,* Ministry Division, 2014. These criteria are the same for everyone and provide the structure and content of a BAP.

2 Yes, because it's policy

1 This assertion of mostly male-led benefices is a function of a roughly 50:50 male/female split for new ordinations for the last three years of available statistics, with 63 per cent of men entering stipendiary ministry but only 39.6 per cent of women. The impact of this weighting is further influenced by the fact that 'female assistant curates are on average five years older than male assistant curates', limiting the time available for them to achieve positions of responsibility before retirement. Some research might well be justified to identify why these differences exist, but that is outside the scope of this book (source: Church of England Statistics for Mission: Ministry, 2010, 2011 and 2012).
2 *Formation for Ministry within a Learning Church: The Structure and Funding of Ordination Training,* the report of a working party set up by the Archbishops' Council, chairman John Hind, April 2003.
3 Amanda Bloor, 'Who shall I be?', in Tim Ling (ed.), *Moving On in Ministry: Discernment for Times of Transition and Change,* London: Church House Publishing, 2013, p. 21.

3 Same old, same old

1 Jane Austen, *Pride and Prejudice,* Chapter 55.
2 Alexander Lowen, *Narcissism: Denial of True Self,* New York: Simon and Schuster, 1985.
3 Wilfred Ruprecht Bion, 1897–1979, an influential British psychoanalyst.
4 James Fowler, *Stages of Faith: The Psychology of Human Development and the Quest for Meaning,* new edition, New York: HarperOne, 1995.
5 M. Scott Peck, *The Different Drum: Community Making and Peace,* New York: Touchstone, 1998.
6 Gerard W. Hughes, *God of Surprises,* London: Darton, Longman and Todd, 2008.

4 One of the gang

1 See Martyn Percy, *Clergy: The Origin of Species,* London: T&T Clark, 2006.

2 The topic of boundaries is explored in detail and with a Christian focus in Henry Cloud and John Townsend, *Boundaries: When to Say Yes, How to Say No, to Take Control of Your Life*, revised edition, Grand Rapids, MI: Zondervan, 2002.

5 I know it's your day off, but . . .

1 David Suchet and Geoffrey Wansell, *Poirot and Me*, London: Headline, 2013, p. 59.

6 The workplace bully

1 Helena Wilkinson, *Insight into Child and Adult Bullying*, Farnham: CWR, 2013.
2 Projective Identification is not to be confused with Transference, which is a far more specific phenomenon. For example, people often talk to doctors, lawyers and professors, not to mention bishops, as if they possess a depth of wisdom and a range of skills, simply by virtue of their titles, that they may not actually have.

7 Working agreement? What working agreement?

1 Diocese of Gloucester outline working agreement.
2 Eric Berne, *Games People Play: The Psychology of Human Relationships*, London: Penguin, 1964.
3 Matthew 5.37, NKJV.

8 Day 200: still at sea

1 The first item in a Statement of Expectations appended to *Good Practice in the Appointment and Training of Training Incumbents*, Ministry Division, 2014.
2 NSMs (non-stipendiary ministers) are now known as SSMs (self-supporting ministers). Although there are exceptions, such individuals generally work in a support capacity and do not have a leadership role in parishes.

A more excellent way

1 Jacqueline Stober writing in *Being a Curate: Stories of What It's Really Like*, ed. Jonathon Ross-McNairn and Sonia Barron, London: SPCK, 2014.

2 2 Corinthians 12.9, KJV.
3 Monica Furlong, 'The Parson's Role Today', paper given at the Wakefield Diocesan Clergy Conference 1966, reproduced in Christopher Perry, *Listen to the Voice Within*, London: SPCK, 1991.

Index

Did you know that SPCK
is a registered charity?

As well as publishing great books by leading Christian authors, we also . . .

. . . make assemblies meaningful and fun for over a million children by running www.assemblies.org.uk, a popular website that provides free assembly scripts for teachers. For many children, school assembly is the only contact they have with Christian faith and culture, and the only time in their week for spiritual reflection.

. . . help prisoners to become confident readers with our easy-to-read stories. Poor literacy is a huge barrier to rehabilitation. Prisoners identify with the believable heroes of our gritty fiction. At the same time, questions at the end of each chapter help them to examine their choices from a moral perspective and to build their reading confidence.

. . . support student ministers overseas in their training. We give them free, specially written theology books, the International Study Guides. These books really do make a difference, not just to students but to ministers and, through them, to a whole community.

Please support these great schemes: visit www.spck.org.uk/support-us to find out more.